THE WORCESTER
LIBER ALBUS

Anno [illegible] CCC. quinto.

[illegible] speciali [illegible] honores [illegible] multiplica [illegible]

[illegible] certissime [illegible] infirmitas [illegible] residentia [illegible]

[illegible]

[illegible] valeat [illegible] differenti [illegible]

[illegible] vestre [illegible]

[illegible] supplicamus [illegible]

[illegible] Valete [illegible] per ces lettres [illegible]

[illegible] Come [illegible] de [illegible]

par le trover sa reparable [illegible]

ces lettres [illegible]

[illegible] chaumbre [illegible]

[illegible]

[illegible] fratri [illegible] Cristi [illegible] humiles [illegible]

[illegible] de Bromesgrave [illegible] papiri [illegible]

[illegible]

[illegible] Anno domini [illegible] CCC quinto [illegible]

[illegible] Prior [illegible]

[illegible] elemosinarie [illegible]

[illegible]

[illegible] Valeat [illegible]

[illegible] Reverendo in Christo patri ac domino domino [illegible] Prior [illegible]

[illegible] humilis [illegible]

[illegible]

Anno domini Millesimo Trecentesimo [illegible]

[illegible] Luna [illegible]

Die Annunciacionis [illegible]

Noverint universi [illegible] de Bromesgrave [illegible]

[illegible]

[illegible] in testimonium sigillum nostrum [illegible]

[illegible]

In die Cene [illegible]

[illegible] Prior [illegible]

[illegible]

[illegible] conserva [illegible]

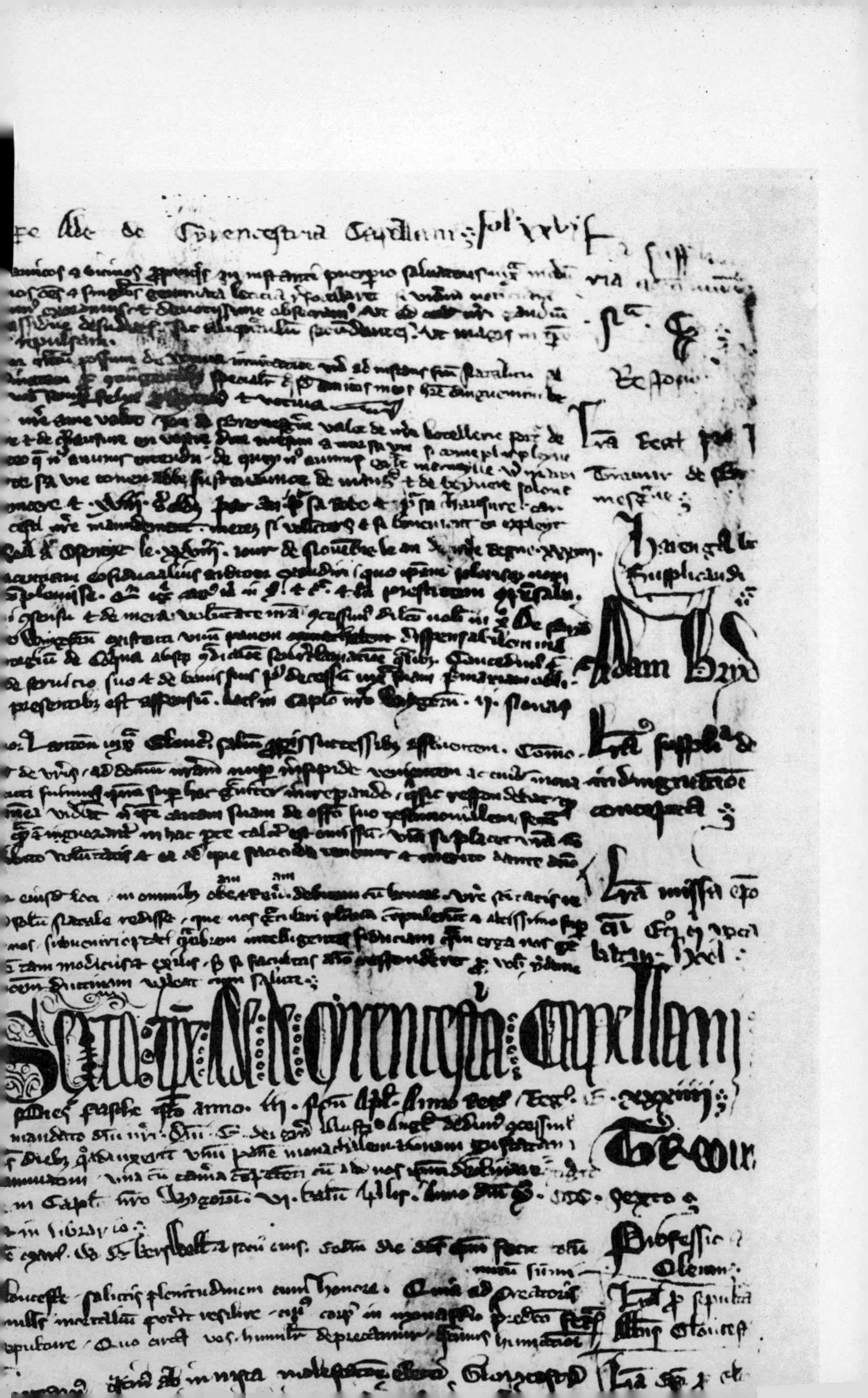

[illegible]

... vostre tres humble chapelein ...

[illegible]

Ade de Cirencestria Capellani

[illegible]

... in Capitulo nostro ... anno domini ...

[illegible]

Facsimile, in the size of the origin[al]

(*From Phot. by Mr. A. Ne*[...]

l, of Folio xxvi. r. of Liber Albus.

ale, Braemar, Worcester).

THE WORCESTER LIBER ALBUS

GLIMPSES OF LIFE IN A GREAT BENEDICTINE MONASTERY IN THE FOURTEENTH CENTURY

BY THE REV.
JAMES M. WILSON, D.D.
CANON AND VICE DEAN

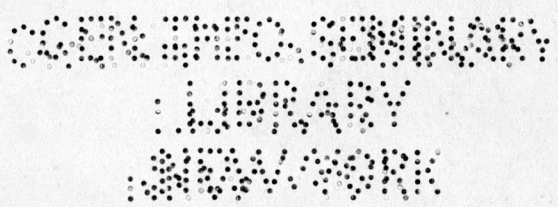

LONDON
SOCIETY FOR PROMOTING
CHRISTIAN KNOWLEDGE
NEW YORK: THE MACMILLAN COMPANY
1920

PRINTED AT THE COMPLETE PRESS
WEST NORWOOD, LONDON

TO THE READER

It is a mad world, my masters, in which the pupil is asked to commend the achievements of his instructors. But that is what is being required of me now.

Some years ago I began to teach myself to decipher the Westminster account-rolls. Dean Armitage Robinson was urging me to it, but declined, quite rightly, to take me seriously, till I had made some progress on my own resources. "Look at Wilson, taking up an entirely new subject at his age! You ought to be ashamed of yourself to let Westminster be left behind." And so on.

Well, in actual fact I did look at Wilson, and derived endless help from his edition of the early Worcester *compoti*; so much so that Dean Armitage Robinson gave me good marks and placed his own immense researches at my disposal.

However, all that is over now, I fear, and here I am presuming to comply with a request from my master that I should say something by way of introduction to his latest labours, though, I am sure, not his last.

Nobody, at any rate, can be more sensible than I of the delight of dealing with a great miscellany like the *Liber Albus*. At Westminster we were in favour of the opposite hue; we had our *Liber Niger Quaternus*. But that was a fifteenth-century production. Canon Wilson's treasure, which he here puts at the reader's disposal, goes back nearer to the great times of the Westminster "Domesday" chartulary (roughly, A.D. 1300).

The difference between studying account-rolls and browsing in a chartulary is the difference between *Principia Latina* in school hours and Fenimore Cooper during an interval. In the one case the method is rigid, and the only hope of a "find" of any interest is to follow the method closely; in the other, you can never tell from page to page upon what exciting adventure you may be launched.

It is in this spirit that, as I hope, the reader will approach the White Book of Worcester in my honoured friend's company, not without a prayer that Canon Wilson may still be spared to the world that he loves and to the many who love him.

ERNEST WORCESTER

THE CASTLE, HARTLEBURY
December 4, 1919

CONTENTS

CONTENTS

CONTENTS

CONTENTS

CONTENTS

INTRODUCTION

ABUNDANT materials exist in print for any one who wishes to study mediæval monastic life in England from original records. Such records have been published under a variety of names in the Rolls Series, and by the Camden and Surtees and other societies; or printed for their subscribers by local historical societies, as Chronicles, Histories of Monasteries, Cartularies, Annals, Lives, Consuetudinaries, Registers, Compotus Rolls, etc. But I know of only one such published Record that has much resemblance to the *Liber Albus* of the Priory of Worcester which furnishes the materials for the present volume. The Record I refer to is the *Literæ Cantuarienses*, edited in 1887 and 1888 for the Rolls Series by the ever-to-be-remembered lover of Canterbury, Dr. Sheppard. That work consists of two 8vo volumes, each of over 500 pages, containing a selection from the documents entered in the Register of the monastery of Christ Church Canterbury by its chancellors. Dr. Sheppard's selection gives nearly 1000 documents, a majority of them being letters, all but the first few bearing dates from A.D. 1320 to 1373. Our *Liber Albus* covers from A.D. 1301 to 1446, and the selection of letters in this volume is taken solely from the years 1301 to 1338.

In each case the materials for selection are the copies, or in some cases perhaps the drafts, of the correspondence of the prior, entered by his chancellor or chaplain, or other official. The *Literæ Cantuarienses* thus gives a picture, to use Dr. Sheppard's words, of "the daily official (and some part of the private) life of a dignitary as high in rank as the head of the oldest Benedictine monastery in England."

Our *Liber* does the same for the head of our great West of England monastery.

But the two books differ nevertheless somewhat widely in the range of their contents. The differences arise from several causes, among which the personality of the priors is perhaps not the least. Our Worcester book is certainly much more varied, and more generally interesting: and it furnishes more details both as to external relations with king and pope and other monasteries, and as to local and personal affairs, than does the Canterbury Register. This latter is both more closely confined to the affairs of its own monastery and it is rather more documentary and official. It also rarely condescends to mention trifles and personalities. In fact, I can only recall one "trifle" in the *Literæ Cantuarienses*. One letter reports the single fact that a messenger, sent to fetch from a bishop some consecrated oil for chrism, got drunk on his return journey and lost his phials, his *ampullæ*.

One can scarcely consider it a "trifle" that the Prior of Christchurch, Canterbury, found that the Prior of Worcester in 1355 had stolen a march on him, and had obtained leave from the Pope to wear mitre, dalmatic, gloves, ring and sandals like those of a bishop, and to give solemn benediction at Mass and at table. It was scarcely a "trifle" that when seated together in provincial councils the Prior of Worcester should be adorned *pluribus ornamentis pontificalibus* than the still greater Prior of Canterbury, and thus publicly inflicted on him *non modicum dedecus*.

But letters like these help to bring the atmosphere of the time before us; and of the two books our *Liber* is the richer in them. Hence I trust that on this, as well as on weightier historical grounds, the present selection will not be deemed superfluous. It is what its title declares it to be. It is not a treatise or an essay; not a register, or history, or customary, or, in fact, anything methodical. It is like a group of lantern slides hopelessly disarranged. It illustrates the many-sidedness of a prior's life; his entanglement in affairs of all kinds; and inferentially it shows something of the place which the Church and Monasticism held at that period in national life, and of the problems they had to solve.

The letters throw light on a great variety of subjects, such as the frequent appropriation of parochial endowments to monasteries, in order to meet their growing expenses; the endowment of vicarages; the founding of chantries, and their relation to the parish churches; papal "provisions," and varied exactions; the demands of the king for subsidies in his Scotch wars; the forced and unsuitable presentations to livings; the many relations, friendly and otherwise, with other monasteries; the state of learning among them; the control exercised by the General Provincial Chapter of the Benedictines; the method of dealing with intolerably disagreeable monks; the corrody-holders, permanent pensioners and often inmates of the convent; besides the legal, financial, landowning, building business of the house.

But I felt it impossible satisfactorily to classify them, and have therefore printed the documents in the order in which they stand in the MS. This plan has the advantage of giving a truer impression of the variety of the life, and the unexpectedness of the incidents as they occur.

The reader will perhaps like to hear something of the MS. itself and its history. The *Liber Albus* is a heavy folio of 497 leaves of vellum of large size, originally bound in boards of white sycamore, whence its name. It was rebound nearly one hundred years ago in white vellum. Until the Dissolution it was in the care of the prior: then along with all the muniments and charters it passed into the hands of the dean and chapter, and was by them entrusted to the chapter clerk. Under his custody it was accessible to historians, but was very rarely read or referred to. The charters were also, alas, accessible; sometimes on very easy and confiding terms; and many hundreds of them, including some of the most valuable, disappeared. In 1907 the *Liber Albus*, with all the ancient muniments and rolls that survived, and the earlier post-Dissolution records, were by chapter order transferred to the Cathedral Library. There they have been catalogued, and some selections printed in the *Transactions of the Worcestershire Historical and Archæological Societies*.

The *Liber* is being also made available to historians in a form entirely different from that of the present volume. The Worcestershire Historical Society has printed in its *Transactions* for 1919 for the use of its members, short abstracts of the first 1286 documents, occupying the first 168 folios of the volume, along with full indices to translations or detailed abstracts of these documents contained in two MS. folios * now placed in our Library. Prefixed to these short abstracts is an Introduction of some length, giving a conspectus of the many departments of the prior's correspondence. It is from these documents, which it was not possible to print in full in the *Transactions*, that a selection has been made for publication in the present volume. It is to be hoped that some future librarian will complete the series of abstracts and indices for the whole volume.

One or two other introductory remarks may be of interest to the reader.

* Add. MSS. 108, 109.

INTRODUCTION

The acting head of the monastery of Worcester is a prior, not an abbot. The bishop was the abbot of his cathedral monastery. But when the bishop ceased to reside in the monastery most of the business passed into the hands of the prior. Convenience and custom and compromise gradually determined the limits of the relative powers and functions of bishop and prior; but there remained some debatable territory; and they watched each other with jealous eyes, ever on the look-out for encroachments.

The fact of Worcester being a cathedral monastery is of the first importance for a right understanding of these letters. The prior and chapter were the bishop's prior and chapter; and to them, therefore, by custom and by canonical law, all sorts of diocesan and episcopal business was referred for sanction. They were the means of communication between the civil and ecclesiastical authorities and the diocese. The Abbots of Gloucester and Pershore, of Evesham and Tewkesbury, were great men; but their letter-books would not show nearly such a variety of interests as that of the Prior of the Cathedral Church of Worcester.

There were doubtless letter-books of the Priors of Worcester earlier in date than this, but they are lost. When this volume opens in 1301 John de Wyke had just been elected prior; Bishop Godfrey Giffard was old, tortured by gout, and nearing the end of his long episcopate. The monastery was in considerable disorder. It had been visited by the diligent Archbishop Robert of Winchelsey early in that year and severely dealt with. The chapter was heavily burdened with debt, and the country was unsettled. The difficulties of the new prior were great. This brief introduction will be, I hope, sufficient to make the letters that follow intelligible and interesting.

It only remains that I should express my obligations to Dr. R. L. Poole for encouragement and occasional assistance in this somewhat arduous work for an amateur like myself; and in particular to Miss Rose Graham, who has revised with knowledge and care many of the MSS. and the proofs of this volume.

JAMES M. WILSON.

How wonderfully they call up the atmosphere of the time! Documents are so invaluable: no history, however brilliant, can produce an equal impression.

Letters of T. E. Brown, vol. ii, p. 61

Each shrine is haunted by the living breath
Of myriad souls, that as they knelt
Poured out into the very stones
Their aspirations, fears, and groans,
And all the pent-up agony they felt,
Part of their living selves that cannot pass,
That mellowing time doth of all evil shrive,
So that the walls themselves become alive
With these their relics, like the hallowing bones
Of saints immured. Their faintly fluttering tones
Vibrate like a perpetual Mass
In rhythmic beat,
Till the entire fabric doth become
From floor to dome
A thing of spirit, immaterial seat
Of the Host High.

"Pilgrims," by Cloudesley Brereton.
Hibbert Journal, October 1918

1

PART OF THE STORY OF JOHN DE DUMBELTON

Folio 1, r. Nos. 1, 2, 9–13, 26, 55, 111, 133, 134. A.D. 1301

[John de Dumbelton was a monk of Worcester at the end of the thirteenth century, and was appointed in 1299 by Bishop Godfrey Giffard to be Prior of Little Malvern. This post he shortly afterwards, in 1301, resigned, and wished to return to the Priory of Worcester. This was much deprecated, as we shall see, by the monks of Worcester on account of his quarrelsome temper.

The prior-elect (John de Wyke) and the Convent of Worcester address Robert (of Winchelsey) the Archbishop of Canterbury.]

"For quiet and the tranquil peace of our fraternity, in which we believe that you take pleasure, graciously allow, if it please you, that John de Dumbelton, late Prior of Little Malvern, whose return we well know would disturb the quiet of our whole community, should stay at our expense in some other house of the same Order; or at least that the Presidents of our General Chapter should arrange for him as they may think best. If your paternity will sanction this, we will obey their orders. We reverently fall at your fatherly feet, and with heartfelt sobs we pour out our earnest prayers, and pray that in this matter you will provide for the salvation of many souls, which in the event of an adverse decision will manifestly be imperilled.

"May your paternity thus feel, as our community feels, that it is better that one man should have his wish frustrated, than that our whole body should perish or be dispersed.

"July 1301."

No. 2. The Archbishop is at Gloucester, and writes to the official of the Bishop of Worcester:

"When we visited the diocese of Worcester we ordered that the Chapter of Worcester should be compelled to admit brother J. de D. as a monk of their house. We therefore strictly order you to admonish and effectually induce the Prior and Convent of the monastery of Worcester to admit him to the position he held before, with all his regular functions.

"If they fail to obey your monitions, or rather mine, proceed by ecclesiastical censure against the greater persons of the monastery as is right; and by your letters patent keep us without delay fully informed as to your action.

"Gloucester, 1301."

No. 9. The Prior and Convent now lay their case more fully before the Archbishop:

"Our former brother and fellow monk lately brought his complaint before the General Provincial Chapter of the Order, asserting that he had unjustly been excluded from his rights as a monk in his own house. He has, however, renounced these rights; he was finally set free from all obedience to the Prior; and was completely transferred to another house, in no relation to ours, and was made its prior. He now seeks to be restored by the Presidents to the position of a monk in our house, preferring as he stated, and as is contained in his petition, that it should be arranged by them and not by you or any one else, and that some secular action for this purpose should be employed.

"Since, therefore, we know that you take pleasure in our quiet life and that of other religious, we devoutly pray you to leave to the said Presidents, whose orders we will as is right obey, the decision as to the status of this man whose return will hinder our holy quiet life, and disturb the minds of the brethren more than it is expedient to state.

"We are ready out of reverence for you, as soon as the matter is finally settled, to provide him with an honourable maintenance in some other house of our Order.

"We beg you to arrange that he should rather be frustrated in his wish, for without obtaining that wish his soul may be sufficiently provided for, than that the salvation of many should be hindered, or that in some other way a greater evil should arise."

No. 10. The Prior and Convent now write to some man of influence, brother W. de Hymuttone. He has been already informed as to the case, and they beg him to prevent J. de D.'s return to Worcester: "Let him return to his priorate of Malvern which he chose; or if no better place can be arranged we will pay for him elsewhere."

No. 11. The Prior writes to a friend unnamed—very confidentially, saying that he has written to the Archbishop, and asking him to use his influence.

No. 12. The Prior writes in the same sense to the Abbot of Westminster, as President of the Order in the province, begging him to order any arrangement for J. de D., "provided that he does not in any measure return to us"; peace and charity will perish; indeed, he believes that some of the brethren will go to other houses. "Better that J. de D. should suffer for his levity and ambition than that the unity of a great community should be shattered."

No. 13. The Presidents of the General Chapter request the Prior and Convent of Worcester to give to J. de D. an allowance of five marks a year to assist him to study at Oxford or elsewhere.

No. 26. The Abbot of Westminster, as one of the two Presidents, urges the Prior and Convent "to conduct yourselves so graciously towards J. de D. that from the Supreme Giver of all good things, the Author of peace and Lover of concord among brethren, you may receive the prize of an eternal reward."

No. 55. The Prior writes to the Abbot of Westminster that though they have sought for J. de D. at Gloucester, Reading, and Malvern, to give him half of the five marks due to him, they could not find him or learn where he was. They are ready to pay to him, or to the President, or any one appointed, and beg to be informed of the decision.

No. 111. The Abbot replies that it should be paid to the Prior at Oxford or Gloucester, lest for want of money J. de D. become a wanderer and outcast—*ne vagus et profugus devenerit.*

The money was sent, but apparently not very graciously. For the next two Presidents, the Abbots of Winchcombe and Pershore, remonstrate with the Prior in 133. But the Prior is impenitent. In 134 he declares that he wrote "*juxta sacræ regulæ patris Benedicti traditiones.*"

He apparently lived generally in Oxford or London, but he visited the monastery occasionally. He manumitted a serf at Tedynton in June 1313, and on the death of the Prior he came to Worcester on October 20, 1317, to vote at the election of his successor, and was resident at Worcester in March 1324 (1023).

THE STORY OF JOHN DE DUMBELTON

He was a learned man. Two books in the Cathedral Library testify to his learning. F. 6, *Novem libri logicæ et philosophiæ Magistri Johannis Dumbleton Monachi Wygorniensis*, and F. 23 also, a treatise on logic. Q. 46 is a volume, which once belonged to him, containing reports of Sermons preached at Oxford about the year 1290.

22

ARREARS OF TITHE FOR THE HOLY LAND. A TYPICAL DEMAND

Folio 2, d. No. 22. A.D. 1301

[Edward I in 1288 had obtained from Pope Nicholas IV a grant of a tenth of Church income for the next six years, for the Holy Land.]

"THE Abbot of Waltham and the Dean of London appointed by the Apostolic See as executors in the matter of the tenths and subventions granted to the Lord Edward, by the grace of God the illustrious King of England, as a subsidy for the Holy Land, to the man of religion, the Lord Prior of the Church of Worcester, Salvation in the Lord.

"We wrote to you some time ago that you should pay to Master Robert Tankard, our subcollector and commissary in these subventions, the sum of £4 17s. 5d. still in your hands out of the total sum of £9 15s. 5$\frac{1}{4}$d., the account rendered at the time by you and the collectors to the venerable fathers J. (John de Pontissera), by the grace of God Bishop of Winchester, and the late O. (Oliver Sutton), Bishop of Lincoln, the executors at that time in the matter of the tenths and subventions: and that you have not cared to satisfy the said Master Tankard as we ordered you, though under pain of canonical distraint we straitly enjoined you to pay him in full the said £4 17s. 5d. before the coming feast of All Saints.

"Otherwise, if further delay occurs, we shall with canonical rigour, place you under ecclesiastical censure, unless reasons are laid before us why this should not take place.

"By the same Master Tankard you are to notify to us, or one of us in London, the days on which you have received these and our former letters, on or before All Souls' Day, by your letters patent containing full details."

Dated, Waltham for the Abbot, and London for the Dean, October 20, 1301.

[This is followed in a few days by a demand from the Abbot of Gloucester. He describes himself as the collector for the city and diocese of Worcester, both of the tenth imposed by the Lord Pope for three years in aid of the Roman Church, and of the tenth granted to the King for six years as a subsidy for the Holy Land. He requests, advises, and exhorts him to pay in time so that he may not be compelled to proceed against him with the rigour of the law. There are also, he notes, arrears amounting to twenty shillings from the fourth year. (Gloucester, November 3, 1301.) He encloses a copy of the commission sent him by R., Bishop of London, and Bartholomew de Ferentino, Canon of London, executors in the matter of the tenth imposed for three years by Boniface VIII in support of the Church of Rome.]

29

LOANS AND DEBTS

Folio 3, d. No. 29. A.D. 1301

[The Prior has borrowed £10 from Robert of Gloucester, Chancellor of Hereford, and begs to be allowed to defer repayment.]

"For your loan of £10, and the patience you have shewn towards us, we and our Convent offer you our sincerest thanks, inadequate indeed, but the best in our power." They are pressed for money, the visit of the King and Queen (19 Ap. 1301) has cost them much, and they have had to pay tenths and fifteenths. But he promises, *dante deo*, to pay at any time that may be named.

[This is a specimen of several such letters. There was a heavy and growing debt on the priory: ready money had to be obtained by borrowing, by selling crops in advance, and, as will be seen later on, by a species of life insurance, promising rations of food during some one's lifetime in return for a sum paid down in cash.]

30

BISHOP GODFREY GIFFARD INVITES THE PRIOR TO DINE WITH HIM

Folio 3, d. No. 30. A.D. 1301

"GODFREY, by Divine permission Bishop of Worcester, to his beloved son in Christ, brother John de Wyke, Prior of Worcester, salvation with the grace and blessing of God.

"On Sunday next after St. Martin's feast day (November 11), come to us, as you love us, at Alvechurch at one o'clock to dine with us on good fat and fresh venison, and an equally fat crane, which chance to have been sent us, and which we do not like to eat without you. It will be a pleasure to us both. Farewell in the Lord."

This was in November 1301. The Bishop of Worcester, Godfrey Giffard, was now an old man. He had been consecrated in 1268. At this time he was an invalid, tortured by gout.

An anonymous letter, in doggish Latin, inserted out of its place as 121, from some clerk friendly to the Prior, and residing with the Bishop, throws some light on this or an earlier invitation. "Do not be vexed, sir," he writes—*non habeatis pro malo*—"or take it amiss that our lord the Bishop has invited your sub-prior and not yourself to dine with him on St. Lawrence's Day (August 10). I have discovered some personal reasons for this which I will briefly state. The Bishop had preconceived something of rancour towards you personally; but he will change this more and more as days go on for affection. He has specially ordered me to write to you, under my own seal, and to request that until the day of the

Assumption of the Blessed Virgin (August 15), you should not come to visit him, nor send him any present. But on that day he specially invites you to his table. My advice is that in this, as in other matters, you should obey his request."

The old Bishop died on January 26, 1302.

The new Prior had, however, previously, in the humblest possible phrases, invited the great Bishop to come to his installation (Folio 3, v. No. 33):

"To the holy father in Christ, and reverend lord, Godfrey, by the grace of God Bishop of Worcester, the most humble of his sons, John, styled Prior of the church of Worcester, obedience on bended knee, and reverence in the Lord, with all that is possible of dutifulness and honour.

"Relying on the sweetness of your fatherhood, we offer you our devout prayers, humbly beseeching you that on Sunday next that follows the feast of St. Matthew, Apostle and Evangelist, on which day, God permitting, our installation will take place, you will, in company if it so please you with the venerable father the Lord of Hereford, graciously be present at our feast, and refresh us and our invited guests by the bounty of your presence. The joy which your lordship's coming will afford will be an honour to us, and will increase many fold the delight of all our guests.

"Write back your will, if it so please you, in this matter; so however that I may not fear a refusal of my request.

"May your paternity long have health in Christ."

31

HAD THE PRIORY SOME LANDED PROPERTY IN IRELAND ?

Folio 3, d. No. 31. A.D. 1301

[This is a curious letter in somewhat doggish Latin, that is to say, English sentences in Latin words, partly a complaint, and partly speaking of cathedral property in Ireland. It is obscure in places.]

"To his masters in Christ, his beloved friends, the Prior and Convent of Worcester, H. de Raggeleye, clerk, commends himself with every wish to please.

"You know, my dearest friends, how some time ago you presented me to the church of Himbleton, and how at my suit you obtained the profession of presenting to it. And now I am surprised that before my resignation or deprivation, without listening to my prayers or examining my rights, you have presented to that church another person. He entered it by a furtive process, and without observing the form of law, deprived me of my goods there, unjustly and contrary to peace, while I was engaged in the King's service in Ireland for matters of public utility and preserving the peace of Christ's faithful people.

"For this reason feeling myself unduly wronged I appeal in these writings for protection to the Apostolic See and the Court of Rome, and seek the Apostles.

"You ought to know, that on the advice of Philip (Aubyn), then your Lord Prior (1286–1296), I handed over the aforesaid church to a certain chaplain to farm for three years at 16 marks a year; and the same Prior pledged himself and his successors for that sum by binding letters which I send you to be inspected and returned to me. Of this money I have received, as far as I recollect, only 40 shillings. The Chaplain has no means of paying, and thus I must have recourse to you.

"Moreover, I have heard that you impute it to me that you have not got possession of your lands in Ireland. You should know that this is not to be imputed to me, and that I have often taken trouble about that business at St. Wulstan's place, near Salmon's Leap, and have incurred much expense. Also I have inquired among the older and more discreet persons in those parts, but I have not been able to find any one who was able to tell me anything of your rights.

"I heard, however, from one talker—*a quodam narratorio*—who lives with the Abbot of Dublin, that he has seen the documents and muniments of that Abbot, and that the Abbot holds those lands you are looking for. And, therefore, you should, if you please, send thither a general attorney, and obtain a writ of both kinds on this matter—*breve utriusque . . . super hiis*.

[There is a blank in the original.]

"If it please you, you may send me your wishes on the matter, so that I may take what further steps seem expedient; and you may feel sure that the lands you are looking for are not at that place which is called St. Wulstan's, near Salmon's Leap, but are in the hilly country near Dublin, where the Abbot of St. Mary's has a certain grange.

"I have often told you this before in my letters; and if you intend to try to get these, you must send a general attorney, who is empowered by the King's writ for gain or loss—*ad lucrandum vel perdendum*.

"He must also obtain a writ from the Chancellor of Ireland to show that those lands are in free alms—

liberæ elemosinæ—for your church or St. Mary's Church, Dublin. And that canon who came to you and said that St. Wulstan's Place, near Salmon's Leap, belonged to your church has left that place, for his want of judgment and malice; and it was from malice, as I have heard, that he said this."

[In the *Annales Wigorniæ*, A.D. 1212, we read that "some one from Ireland, whose tongue had been cut out when he was three years old, was healed at the tomb of St. Wulstan (Wulstan was canonized in 1203). In return for this miracle this gentleman, by name Pippard, built a large church in Ireland in honour of St. Wulstan, Bishop and Confessor, and gave the aforesaid place to the Church of Worcester along with thirty carucates of land." From *Liber Albus* 562 we learn that the name of the place was Clanculum.

Mr. Alfred de Burgh, Assistant Librarian of Trinity College, Dublin, has very kindly supplied the following note:

"St. Wolstan's is situated on the south-east side of the River Liffey, between Leixlip and Celbridge, in Co. Kildare. 'The priory of St. Wolstan's was founded in the year 1202 for canons of the Order of St. Victor, by Richard, first Prior of the place, and Adam de Hereford, in memory of St. Wolstan, Bishop of Worcester, then newly canonized.' 'The remains of the priory consist of two gateways, a tower, and two fragments.' These are marked on the Ordnance Survey Map, and photographs of them and of the later dwelling-house in 1792 are given in an account of the family of Sir John Alen, Chancellor of Ireland, to whom the priory was granted in 1536, and in another article on St. Wolstan's, in vols. iv (1903–1905) and ii (1896–1899) of the *Journal of the Co. Kildare Archæological Society*.

"A history of the priory is given by Mr. Archdall in his *Monasticon Hibernicum* (Dublin, 1786).

"Leixlip is the Danish translation of the name Salmon Leap, a cataract on the Liffey above the present village, about twelve miles west of Dublin. Giraldus Cambrensis, after speaking of the fish leaping up the cataract, says, 'Hence the place derives its name of Saltus salmonis.'

"Clanculum is probably Glencullen, properly described as 'in the hilly country near Dublin.' Glencullen is a valley about four miles long, eight miles south of Dublin, and twelve miles from Leixlip. It lies between Tibradden and Two Rock Mountains on the north-east, and Cruagh and Glendoo Mountains on the south-west.

"It is a very beautiful mountain valley, narrow under the steep slope of Tibradden at its western end, but expanding to a width of a couple of miles farther east. At present the narrow part is planted with fir, and the eastern half occupied by mountain farms and granite quarries.

"The last of the Alens connected with St. Wolstan's was an officer in the Irish Brigade at Fontenoy in 1745. He was called in France the Count de St. Wolstan. His Irish property was confiscated, and sold in 1752 to Dr. Robert Clayton, Bishop of Clogher, who bequeathed it to his niece Anne, wife of Dr. Thomas Bernard, Bishop of Killaloe. During the later years of the eighteenth century and beginning of nineteenth century, St. Wolstan's was a school kept by John Coyne. In 1822 it was bought by the grandfather of Colonel Claude Cane, the present owner.

"I do not know where the Abbot of St. Mary's had his grange. The prior of the Holy Trinity (Christ Church Cathedral) had his grange—still called Dean's Grange—on the flat land between the Two Rock Mountain and the sea, below the eastern entrance to the valley Glencullen.

"The word glen appears often in old documents as clan, and the cottagers who now live in the valley call it Glancōōlan."

For description and history see a paper by Colonel R. Claude Cane in the *Journal of the Royal Society of Antiquaries of Ireland*, Series vi, vol. ix, June 30, 1919.]

43

QUEEN MARGARET REQUESTS THE PRIOR TO ADMIT A CERTAIN MONK

Folio 4, d. No. 43. A.D. 1301

" MARGARET, by the grace of God Queen of England, Lady of Ireland, Duchess of Aquitaine, to the men of religion, beloved by her in Christ, the Prior and Convent of Worcester, salvation and sincere affection in Christ.

" We intend to augment the pile of our merits by procuring that to one who desires, for his salvation's sake, to devote himself to Divine worship in the habit of a Regular, a path shall be opened for the attainment of his wish.

" Since then our beloved in Christ, Roger de Styvintone, a relative of our beloved Master J. de Kenle, physician—*phisicus*—to our lord the King, whom from our affection for him, as his merits deserve, we regard with benevolence and favour, longs above all else for the sweetness of that Divine worship which is piously and honestly offered in your house and will edify him to salvation, and desires therefore to serve the Lord in your community in the habit of a Regular, we earnestly beg and request your devotion, and we pray that you will admit the said Roger, as your fellow-monk and brother ; so that in addition to the Divine reward thereafter to be conferred on you we ourselves may be more sincerely bound to you.

" Reply by the bearer of these presents what you shall decide to do in this matter."

[Entry into such a monastery as that of Worcester was a coveted privilege. A standard of birth and character and attainments was maintained, as we see from later letters.]

53

THE ARCHBISHOP RESTRICTS THE HOSPITALITIES CLAIMED FROM THE MONASTERIES BY OFFICIALS OF THE BISHOP

Folio 5, d. No. 53. A.D. 1301

[A long letter of which the following is an abstract.]

" ROBERT by Divine permission Archbishop of Canterbury, Primate of all England, to the men of religion, the Abbots of the monasteries of Winchecombe and Pershore, and the Rector of the Church of Cleeve, of the diocese of Worcester, salvation, grace, and benediction.

" That man deserves to be treated as unworthy of liberality who in return for kindnesses that he has received at no expense to himself—*gratuitis*—strives to impose on his benefactor."

The Archbishop had found in his recent visitation that the hospitality which had been shown by the monasteries to the Bishop and his predecessors, voluntarily and out of mere liberality, had come to be claimed as a right by the Bishop's officials. This was the case at Worcester, Gloucester, Lanthony, Bristol, and Cirencester. " When consistory courts were held there or in the adjacent towns, even against the wishes and protests of the religious, the officials remained for three, four, or often for eight days entirely at the cost of the monastery, to their prejudice and serious injury. These facts were quite notorious. Judges have no such rights to demand hospitality, and it is the duty of the Archbishop to relieve those who are unjustly oppressed. He therefore in that visitation ordered that the official of the Bishop and his successors and other servants—*ministri*—of the Bishop were to be restrained from unjustly imposing burdens of this sort on the religious." He similarly forbids the religious to receive within their precincts the officials or any ministers of the Bishop, when attending consistory or other courts, at the expense of the house. They need not, however, cease to show honour to the official and other ministers by sending them presents—*in exenniis mittendis*.

The prohibition is repeated in full, *sub pena excommunicationis majoris quam ex nunc in contravenientes proferimus in hiis scriptis*.

56

SOME SCENES WHEN GODFREY GIFFARD LAY DYING

Folio 6, d. No. 56. December 1301 and January 1302

"To their distinguished friend, if they may so address him, J. de Langton, Chancellor of the illustrious King of England, the Prior and Convent of the Church of Worcester, send all friendship and reverence and honour.

"We understand that you may have heard that our Lord Bishop is under bond to the King for more than 1000 marks, on account of men who have escaped from his prison. He is now *in extremis*, and there is no hope of his life. Yet his people, by their own orders, are now selling, removing, dispersing and wasting all his moveable property; so that on his death little or nothing will be found to meet the King's demands. The bishopric will therefore be irrecoverably burdened. His woods, fish-ponds (*vivaria*), and parks are also being destroyed in most deplorable fashion.

"We most earnestly request your lordship, as our special and trusted refuge, to arrange that some speedy and effective assistance may be found for the interests of our lord the King in the distress of the bishopric of Worcester, and of the Bishop who will succeed to it. Please to let us know your will in this matter."

In (61) we have the orders from the Archbishop to the Abbot of Winchcombe, and the official of the Archdeacon of Worcester, to see that the plundering is stopped and the stolen property restored.

57

A CHARGE AGAINST GODFREY GIFFARD

Folio 6, r. No. 57. A.D. 1302

[This letter is addressed by the Prior John de Wyke either to a clerk of the Chancellor, or to a chaplain or the official of the Archbishop, in January 1302. The Bishop Godfrey Giffard, had obtained the Pope's authority to levy first-fruits from the diocese for three years for the repair of the cathedral church and its buildings: and it was alleged that he had not applied the money for that purpose. For further detailed charges and the Bishop's reply, see Thomas, Worcester Cathedral, Appendix, pp. 66–71.]

"To his special and learned friend the Prior of Worcester, with great affection.

"Our lord the Bishop is now lying in such extreme sickness that there is no hope of his life. You know that through the privilege granted him of receiving first-fruits, he has received a large, indeed a very large, amount of money: but of this he has contributed or expended nothing at all on the fabric of the Church of Worcester, although the first-fruits were granted him for that purpose. Indeed, on the Episcopal houses he has not spent 60 marks. The woods also which belong to the bishopric, his fish-ponds (*vivaria*), and game, have been so wasted and spoiled through the neglect of the Bishop and his agents, that the Church has suffered through him an immense and irrecoverable loss.

"Moreover, he owes to our lord the King, on account of the escape of some prisoners, more than a thousand marks sterling: and his servants are everywhere without ceasing selling and carrying off all his chattels and live stock, so that after his death nothing will remain to compensate this loss to the church and the bishopric.

"We make therefore the most earnest appeal to you that by ordering a sequestration and issuing a timely notice, a remedy as to that matter of first-fruits, which is understood to be in the hands of your master, may be provided by your master for our loss and that of the Church of Worcester, with all possible haste and speed, and that you will let us know by your reply your decisions on all these matters."

58

THE ARCHBISHOP ORDERS THE REMOVAL OF THE TOMB IN THE CATHEDRAL WHICH BISHOP GODFREY GIFFARD HAD PREPARED FOR HIMSELF

Folio 6, d. No. 58. A.D. 1301

"ROBERT, by Divine permission Archbishop of Canterbury, etc., to the Prior and Sacrist, etc.

"When lately we were, in the discharge of our duty, personally visiting your church we found that our venerable brother Godfrey, by the grace of God Bishop of Worcester, had erected a great monument for his own burial, quite close to the great altar of the church, above the spot where stands the shrine of St. Oswald; and that it has certain pinnacles upon it constructed after the fashion of a tabernacle—a lofty and sumptuous erection of carved stone.

"Moreover, the venerable body of one who is commonly counted as a saint, John de Constantiis, which even after a hundred years and more has not yet crumbled into dust, but is still exposed to view whole and entire, for this purpose has been, to its dishonour, along with the coffin which contained it, removed from the place where it used to rest and be venerated by the people. This tomb along with that of the Bishop aforesaid occupies the place in which according to the custom of other churches *sedilia* should be prepared for the priest and other ministers of the altar, with a view to the celebration of Masses. It improperly prevents sufficient light from falling from the natural quarter upon the altar; and other inconveniences are commented on by the public—*a vulgo*—which it would be unbecoming here to mention.

"It rests on our shoulders, and it is our wish, to care for both the honour and safety of the Church, and to remove the scandal which we find has arisen, having as much regard for the honour of our venerable brother as is possible. We therefore order that the monument with the structure above indicated shall be removed from that spot and placed lower down; and be erected with sufficient honour, at some distance, but near that spot, on its south side, where it may be more plainly seen by those who pass by. The body of the aforesaid saint is to be replaced where it was before; and *sedilia* are to be prepared. In order that these our commands may be duly carried out, to the greater beauty of the house of the Lord, the honour of God, and for the more decent burial of the Bishop when the Creator so orders, we straitly charge and command you in virtue of your obedience, and under pain of canonical compulsion, that within eight days of the receipt of this letter, you direct under our authority that this monument and the whole fabric aforesaid shall be entirely taken down—*demoliri*—and its site be restored to its former condition, suitable and necessary for the ministers at the altar.

"You are, moreover, to convey a message to the Bishop that he may direct that his tomb shall be constructed on the lower spot mentioned above, if he pleases, or in some other more suitable position where it neither obstructs the light, nor prejudices the convenience or beauty of the church in any respect.

"We should aim, in fact, by a dignified and beautiful funeral of our Bishop to enhance the greatness of the church, in such a way that those who minister therein should suffer no disadvantage therefrom. Should there be opposition and resistance, you will quell it canonically by any ecclesiastical severity, and you will duly certify us as to your action in this matter when opportunity occurs.

"Given at Mayfield, January 10, A.D. 1302, in the eighth year of our consecration."

The Prior's reply is given in (88), dated February 12, 1302:

"To the Archbishop, etc., John, humblest in the number of his sons, Prior of the cathedral church of Worcester, falling humbly before his feet.

"For the fact that hitherto we have not caused the tomb of our father Bishop Godfrey, lately deceased, to be removed pray deign, with your usual compassion, kindly to hold us excused. For by reason of our fear of the imminent death of our father, which at least in popular opinion would have been thereby hastened, and in order to avoid a public scandal, relying on your kindness we postponed doing it at the time. It can be more properly done, however, if you wish, after the body is reduced to dust."

64

THE PRIOR'S DUTIES. *SEDE VACANTE*

Folio 7. Nos. 64 *et seq.* and 101

When the See of Worcester fell vacant, by an agreement made in 1268 between Boniface, Archbishop of Canterbury, and the Convent, the Prior was appointed the official of the Archbishop; and this appointment conferred on him extensive powers, and as a result of using those powers, large fees also. The documents following on the death of Godfrey Giffard show that the Prior lost no time. The Bishop died on January 26. On the 27th the Prior sends the sub-Prior and Sacrist to secure the official seal of the Bishop, his register, and all the instruments, charters, privileges, muniments, books, chalices, ornaments, etc., belonging to the Church of Worcester. On the 28th he instructs the official of the Archdeacon to convene all the abbots, priors, deans, provosts, preceptors, and masters of the monasteries, churches, colleges, and hospitals, and all the rural deans and their apparitors to appear before him in the cathedral and profess obedience. This includes all who held vicarages, chantries, portions, etc. On the same day a long list of rectors and others known to be contumacious or owing fines are to be summoned or excommunicated. On the 29th the rolls and registers of the Consistory Courts of Worcester, Gloucester, and Bristol are sent for. On the 30th he requests the Archbishop to appoint him as his official according to the ancient agreement. On the 31st he instructs rural deans to notify his visitation of parishes. All rectors, vicars, priests, with their clerks and ministers, and four trustworthy laymen, from each church and chapel, are to attend. On the same day he instructs the rural deans of adjacent deaneries that all their clergy are to attend him in the cathedral. A little later followed a summons to all who hold any ecclesiastical office, or receive any pension, to bring their authorities—*suas dispensationes et munimenta, ac jus speciale, si quod habeant, quorum aut cujus virtute, personatus, dignitates, ecclesias, portiones, pensiones, seu beneficia hujusmodi se asserunt optinere*; also all non-resident vicars and chantry priests are summoned, and all who have been admitted to benefices since the Council of Lyons, and have failed within a year of their admission to take priest's orders. Later still follows the notice of visitation of monasteries.

68

PROCEEDINGS ON THE DEATH OF THE BISHOP

Folio 8, d. No. 68. A.D. 1302

[Immediately on the death of Godfrey Giffard the Prior and Convent request the King to grant them leave to elect his successor. The letter is as follows.]

" To the most excellent prince and their lord, Edward, by the grace of God the illustrious King of England, Lord of Ireland, and Duke of Aquitaine, his devoted brother J., Prior of the Cathedral Church of Worcester, and the Chapter of the same place, salvation in Him by whom kings reign with every reverence and honour.

" By these present letters we intimate to your excellency that the Lord Godfrey, of good memory, sometime Bishop of Worcester, has entered on the way of all flesh. Wherefore, lest the church should remain longer deprived of the solace of its pastor, we send to the height of your loftiness—*ad celsitudinis vestræ culmen*—our brethren and fellow-monks, humbly praying that you will concede to us licence to elect.

" May your royal sublimity and your empire be increased to the honour of the Most High for many years to come."

To this letter the King replied on February 20, granting their request, and " ordering them to elect as their bishop and pastor one who is devout towards God, capable of ruling your church, and useful and faithful to us and our realm."

They elected John de St. German. How his election was disapproved by the Archbishop as informal, though approved by the King, and not confirmed by the Pope, must be read elsewhere.

74

INQUIRY AS TO THE FITNESS OF A CLERK TO BE INSTITUTED TO A BENEFICE

Folio 8, d. No. 74. A.D. 1302

[It may be interesting to give in full the instruction given by the Prior, *sede vacante*, to the Archdeacon to inquire as to the fitness of a presentee.]

"The men of religion, the Prior and Convent of Great Malvern, have presented to us Master Adam Aubrey of Brecknock, Clerk, for the church of Upton-juxta-Snodsbury, which is vacant, and, as is stated, is in their gift. We, therefore, order you to inquire or make diligent inquiry to be made, concerning his condition, conversation, orders, birth, and age; whether he holds any dignity, office, or other benefits or benefices, with cure of souls; and on other matters which affect his personal fitness. You should also inquire whether the said church is legally vacant, and at what date and in what manner the vacancy began; and whether it is *de facto* vacant: whether it is charged with a pension, and if so to whom and what amount; whether it is involved in any lawsuit; and also whether the said Prior and Convent are the true patrons of the church, and presented to it on the last occasion; and on other points usually and rightfully considered in such a matter. The inquiry should be made in full chapter of the place through men worthy of trust who have full knowledge of the truth in the foregoing matters, etc."

96

HOW MONEY WAS COLLECTED FOR THE EXPENSES OF BUILDING AND REPAIRING THE CATHEDRAL

Folio 11, r. No. 96. A.D. 1302

[References to building operations are extremely rare in the records of the monastery. Hence this letter is of exceptional interest. It is written by the Prior, John de Wyke, acting, *sede vacante*, as the Bishop.]

"THE Prior of the Cathedral Church of Worcester, bearing the care, office and administration of spiritual matters in the diocese of Worcester, during the vacancy of the See, to archdeacons, officials, deans, abbots, priors, rectors, vicars, chaplains, and other ecclesiastical persons, and the whole body of the faithful settled in the diocese of Worcester, salvation in the Son of the Glorious Virgin.

"Following in the footsteps of the venerable fathers of happy memory, Walter, Godfrey, and others presiding over the church of Worcester, and wishing to invite your devotion to assist in works of mercy, we have thought good, with the advice of our chapter, with a view to the salvation and the healing of souls, to revive the old established *confraria* of the mother church of Worcester.

"We, therefore, entreat all of you—*universitas*—and implore you in the Lord, that when the messengers of this *confraria* shall come to you to ask for the alms of the faithful in aid of the work of building the church of Worcester, you will out of your charity admit them with kindness, and treat them with courtesy.

"And you, rectors, vicars and chaplains of parishes, take pains by exhortation in your words, and by example of your good deeds, diligently and effectually to induce those who are under your charge to have their names inscribed in the said *confraria* : and that from the goods which God has conferred upon them, they should, as God has inspired in their minds, contribute to this fund in their lifetime ; and at their death, for the salvation of their souls, leave gifts to it. Let them be assured that whoever gives of his charity anything from his goods to the said *confraria* after confession and with true penitence, may know that the third part of any penance laid upon him is remitted, and, moreover, that there have been granted by the most holy father the Lord Pope, and from the venerable father the Archbishop and Bishop, 1028 days of indulgence.

" We grant also that all benefactors to the building work of the church of Worcester shall share in all the prayers and benefits which are offered in that church, and in the whole diocese for ever.

" Moreover, if a church to which a messenger from the church of Worcester has come on this business is by diocesan or archidiaconal authority placed under an interdict, that interdict will be relaxed on that day.

" The bodies also of the dead, by whatever death they may have died (unless they have been by name and specially excommunicated), whose names are found in the book of the *confraria*, may be buried in the cemetery and in consecrated ground, unless there is some reasonable objection.

" The collections in each parish church should be handed to the bearer of these presents, on the appointed day and at the appointed place, without any condition or demur or diminution.

" We, therefore, strictly enjoin and command you, all and singly, for the remission of your sins, and in virtue of your holy obedience, that you admit no *confraria* or other collectors of any kind until the said *confraria* of our church of Worcester has been attended to; but that you generously give precedence, with all reverence, to the messengers of our church over all other collectors at least from the time of their arrival till after Easter in every year.

"In testimony whereof our seal is appended.

"Worcester, 1302."

Note.—In the *Annales Monastici*, Vol. IV, Rolls Series, p. 417, under the year 1224 we read *Confraternitas hujus ecclesiæ incepit in Januario die S. Wulstani duratura per septennium.*

99

THE PURGATION OF A HOMICIDE

Folio 11, d. No. 99. A.D. 1302

[This is an interesting illustration of the law at that time. The *Sede Vacante Register* (Willis Bund), pp. 93–5, should be compared. For the procedure see Pollock and Maitland, *History of English Law*, pp. 443–4; and Rashdall, *Universities of Europe*, ii, pp. 410, 457.]

"THE official of Worcester, *sede vacante*, to the man of discretion the official of the Archdeacon of that place, or of his deputy, salvation in the Author of salvation.

"Since Thomas le Deyre of Gloucester, clerk, for the crime of homicide and other crimes, was tried before the judges of our lord the King, and by lay judgment—*laycale judicium*—and was then condemned to death; and subsequently, in accordance with ecclesiastical liberty and the approved custom of the realm, was committed—*mancipatus*—to the prison of our Lord Bishop of Worcester at Worcester; and since we on the evidence of trustworthy persons concerning his life, and honourable character, and innocence, have conceived a very strong presumption of his innocence; we have assented to humble petitions sent us, and have decreed that he shall be purged from these charges as justice requires.

"We, therefore, commit it to you, and in virtue of your obedience we straitly charge you that in solemn places, churches, and places in the said archdeaconry, and especially in markets, meetings, and hundreds, you cause to be publicly announced and proclaimed, and see that a notice of public citation be put forward, that if there are any who desire peremptorily to oppose that purgation they are to appear before me or my deputy in the cathedral church of Worcester on the Monday next before the feast of St. Ambrose, Bishop (April 4), to reason and teach wherefore his purgation ought not to be proceeded with, and do what is in agreement with law and reason.

"What you shall have done in the foregoing matter you are to certify us or our deputy at the time or place named, distinctly and openly by your letters patent, giving all details.

"Given at Worcester, February 25, 1302."

109

A LETTER (ANONYMOUS) IN DOG LATIN TO A PERSON IN CHARGE OF NOVICES

Folio 13, d. No. 109. A.D. 1302

[As a curiosity in Latin I transcribe this letter, and submit a translation partly due to Dr. R. L. Poole.]

"AMICO suo in temptatione probato suus possessus salutem bonam ut sibi. Superiorem compellere nequeo ad committendum personæ capaci petita, quod displicet mihi valde; sed unum scio, quod in brevi novicii sentient relevamen optatum. Penitet me primariam vestram petitionem admitti non posse scribentis impotentia duntaxat causante, cum secundum jura nullus poterit factum promittere alienum. De negotiis possibilibus socium vestrum probate; de impossibilibus sustinete, si libet. Valete in regimine angelorum vestrorum quos novicios appellatis."

"For his friend, proved such in time of trial, his devoted servant wishes good health as he would wish for himself.

"I cannot force my superior to entrust my request to a capable person. At this I am much vexed; but one thing I know that the novices will soon feel the desired relief. I am sorry that your first request cannot be granted, solely by reason of my incompetency as a writer, while by rights no one can promise performance by any one else. Test your friend in things he can do; in what he cannot do, bear with him if you please. All success in the management of those angels of yours whom you call novices!"

138

AN INDULGENCE OFFERED BY THE BISHOP WILLIAM OF GAINSBOROUGH

Folio 16, r. No. 138. A.D. 1303

[The Bishop was a Franciscan; and it will be noticed that he associates St. Francis with SS. Wulstan and Oswald.]

"To all the sons of holy Mother Church whom this letter shall reach, brother William, by Divine permission Bishop of Worcester, eternal salvation in the Lord.

"We hold that we perform a duty acceptable and pious towards God when by the attractive gifts of indulgence we stir the minds of the faithful to devout prayer. We, therefore, trusting in the mercy of Almighty God, of the glorious Virgin His Mother, of the blessed Apostles Peter and Paul, and of the holy confessors Francis, Wulstan, and Oswald, and in the merits of all the saints, offer in our compassion to all our parishioners, and to others whose diocesans accept this our indulgence as valid, who, after true penitence and confession, for the soul of Matilda Hervers de Wyke, formerly the wife of Roger of Walcote, whose body rests interred in the cemetery of the monks of Pershore, and to all who for the peace and tranquillity of Church and King and Realm, and the souls of the faithful departed, shall with devout mind say the Lord's Prayer with the Angelic Salutation, forty days of relaxation from penance imposed on them.

"In testimony whereof our seal is hereto appended.

"Given at Kempsey, September 26, 1303."

[It will be noticed that the letters of the Bishop of Worcester are dated from many places. They had manors and houses at Hartlebury, Alvechurch, Wick Episcopi, Kempsey, Bredon, and Hampton Episcopi, as appear from the volume.]

140

THE ARCHBISHOP CERTIFIES THAT THE WORCESTER MUNIMENTS ARE SATISFACTORY

Folio 16, d. No. 140. A.D. 1303

" Robert, Archbishop, etc.

" After seeing, inspecting, and diligently examining your instruments and muniments relating to the appropriations of churches, seculars, tithes, portions and pensions which you hold and receive in your own and alien churches and their parishes in the diocese of Worcester, in which by our metropolitical rights we exercise the office of visitation, we by our office give you discharge as sufficiently protected—*munitos*—in this respect.

" Gloucester, July 27, 1303."

[This inspection probably took place in 1301 on the occasion of the Archbishop's visitation of the monastery. The muniments were again inspected on April 30, 1317, by the official of Hereford as the deputy of the Archbishop, *custos* of the spiritualities, *sede vacante*, with special reference to the appropriation of Lindridge, and the convent was found to be *sufficienter munitos*.]

141

WILLIAM OF GAINSBOROUGH VISITS THE CONVENT

Folio 16, d. No. 141. A.D. 1303

[The new Bishop, William of Gainsborough, wrote (132) from Hampton on September 3 to give notice of his intended visitation. " All are to be present, and to receive us with due reverence and honour."]

" MEMORANDUM that on Thursday next after the feast of St. Matthew Apostle and Evangelist, that is to say on the 6th of the Kalends of October, the dominical letter being *F*, Lunæ XII, *anno Domini* 1303, and in the 31st year of the reign of King Edward, son of King Henry, William of Gainsborough, Bishop of Worcester, visited the Prior and Chapter of Worcester in such manner as follows :

" In the first place he entered with clerks and seculars, and preached. And this was his Thema : 'I descended into my garden.' When this was finished, his clerks and ours discussed a certain new constitution, which the Pope had recently put forth, respecting the entrance of a bishop for making a visitation. And since it was doubted whether that decretal was common or special, general or local, the Prior made protest that he would admit him on that occasion with two clerks and one notary, always, however, saving our composition if that constitution was not general. The Bishop made a like protest ; and the clerks who entered and were with the Bishop in the said visitation were Master Walter of Wotton, Archdeacon of Huntingdon ; Master John of Rodborough, and Master John Caleys, notary public.

" On the first day of the visitation he dined with the Prior in the Guest Hall—*aula hospitum*—and as he could not complete his work on the first day, he visited similarly on the second day with his clerks almost till the ninth hour. He dined on that day at Kempsey."

Note 1. The text on which the Bishop preached is Cant. vi. 11. "I went down into the garden of nuts, to see the green plants of the valley, to see whether the vine budded, and the pomegranates were in flower."

Note 2. Dr. Poole refers to Boniface VIII's decretal concerning procurations at a visitation. *Corp. Juris. Canon.*, VI, Lib. III; Tit. xx. 3.

[The Bishop again visited the monastery (367) in August 1306. Another visitation is reported (1198) by Bishop Montacute in 1334.]

160

A COMMISSION APPOINTED BY THE BISHOP TO INQUIRE WHETHER THE PRIOR WAS REGULARLY APPOINTED

Folio 17, d. Nos. 160, 161, 170. A.D. 1303

[This is one of the incidental difficulties that arose between the Bishop and the Prior and the Convent.]

"WILLIAM, by Divine permission Bishop of Worcester, to our beloved in Christ, Master John of Rodborough, and Walter of Wotton, salvation, grace, and benediction.

"On a reported defect in appointment brought against John de Wyke, now Prior of our cathedral church of Worcester, on the occasion of the recent visitation we held in the chapter house of the said church, we commit our powers to you, jointly and severally, after understanding the merits of the case, and weighing all that ought to be weighed, to decide as shall seem just."

161

THE DECISION

"In the name of God, Amen.

"Since recently, at the visitation held by our venerable father William, by the grace of God Lord Bishop of Worcester, in the chapter house of his cathedral church, it was objected against John de Wyke, now Prior of the said church, that his entrance to the post of the said priorate was officially faulty, after hearing the reply of the said Prior who firmly asserted that his entrance was canonical, and having fully understood the merits of the case and weighed all that had to be weighed, we, John of Rodborough, Clerk, special commissary of the said father for this business, considering that the entrance of the said Prior on the post of the said priorate was canonical, with the authority committed to us pronounce that the Prior is, so far as pertains to the office of the said father, free from all imputation.

"This pronouncement was read aloud from the writing, by me John of Rodborough, the commissary aforesaid, in the chapter house of the monks of the church of Worcester on the Monday after the feast of St. Thomas the Apostle, A.D. 1303, in the presence of the said Prior and Convent therein assembled, and also of the men of discretion, Walter of Wotton, Archdeacon of Huntingdon; Geoffrey of Northwick, W. of Gloucester, clerks; John de Caleys and John of Broadwas, notaries-public, seeing and hearing that these things so took place.

"In testimony of all which things my seal is affixed."

[There was a mystery about this suggestion of an irregularity in the appointment of the Prior.

In 170 we have a letter from the Prior to the Bishop, in substance, as follows.]

170

"May God reward your recent devout labours in quelling this discord that has arisen.

"The excommunication pronounced in our chapter against all concerned in the malicious abstraction and concealment of my letters of appointment has had the effect of securing their restoration from persons outside. Some of my brethren have with great sorrow confessed to me." The Prior, therefore, asks for power of absolution for this wrong, and also for any irregularity that may have occurred from their celebrating Mass when under sentence.

Dated February 25, 1304.

[In the margin is a note to the effect that these letters were brought back to the Prior by brother J. de Cestenlade, of the Order of Preachers, in the convent at Gloucester, on February 20, 1303–4.]

162

MONKS CAUGHT IN A STORM

Folio 17, d. No. 162. A.D. 1303

[A trifling incident; but preserved in the *Liber Albus*. Some monks had gone out for a long walk, probably to Malvern; were caught in a storm; took refuge in Malvern Priory, and stayed the night there.]

"We had pleasure in entertaining our dear brothers your fellow-monks, who turned aside to us yesterday on account of the stormy weather. As we should wish our brethren to be entertained by any Catholic, most of all by those who hold the faith of our house, we pray your Reverence that of your gracious piety you will pardon their not returning at the hour appointed. Farewell."

167

AN ANNUAL TRIBUTE OF FIFTY PAIRS OF SLIPPERS

Folio 18, r. No. 167. A.D. 1304

It is a curious glimpse into a world that has passed away to read, in 167, a letter from the Prior to the Abbot of the Cistercian convent of Bordesley, claiming 50 pairs of slippers, to be worth at least fourpence a pair—about five shillings or more of our money.

The letter is as follows:

"To the man of holy religion, and my beloved friend in Christ, P., by the grace of God Abbot of Bordesley, brother J., Prior of the monastery of Worcester, with sincere charity in the Lord.

"The letter of obligation of yours which we hold, the tenor of which being public and notorious we do not believe to have escaped your memory and that of your convent, speaks very plainly of our presentation of two clerks to be admitted as monks in your monastery at successive dates, and in like manner of your annual presentation of 50 pairs of slippers, the value of each pair being at least 4 pence, to our almoner for the soul of the late Sampson of Bromsgrove, to be performed for ever on the day of his anniversary. It mentions also the fine of 100 shillings to be sent as often as there is a failure to make the aforesaid payment.

"We, therefore, being in possession of the aforesaid proofs, and being desirous to carry out the wholesome wish of the deceased, as far as lies in our power, request in the Lord your holiness, as we have done before, that in order to avoid both the fines imposed on such defaulters by the statutes of our lord the King, and the fine stated in your submission above mentioned, you will make a virtue of necessity—*faciendo de necessitate virtutem*—and will be pleased to give orders respecting the 50 pairs of slippers owing for the year, that satisfaction be made to our almoner who is in difficulty about them; so that others of the faithful may be the more moved to similar pious offerings, and that you and we may henceforth enjoy greater peace of mind.

"March 19, 1303."

178

TESTIMONIAL TO AN ASPIRANT FOR MONASTIC LIFE

Folio 18, d. No. 178. *Circa* A.D. 1304

[The following letter shows that boys were occasionally brought up and educated in the monastery and passed on into religious life.]

"To the men of religion devoted to God, and our beloved in Christ, the Lord Prior of Great Malvern, and the venerable company of the same place, brother John, Prior of Worcester, with close fraternal charity, greeting.

"At the earnest and frequent request made to us and to others by John de Maddeley, clerk, a man of high merit in life, learning and character, and in the flower of his age, one whom almost from infancy our house has brought up, we affectionately request you of your charity and urged thereto by our request, to be willing to admit the youth into the habit as a brother. He earnestly desires to serve his Creator, under regular observances, in your monastery. We hope that his companionship, now that his probation as a boy is past, for the fervency of the love he bears to your house above all others, will be to you a source of pleasure."

[This letter was accompanied by a private letter from the Sacrist, John de Harley, recommending J., and another clerk, R., as well deserving and fit *pro monachali observantia regulari*. The Abbot will be able *conditiones et merita explorare*. *In mea reputatione reperientur ydonei ordinis oneri*.

The Prior also writes and reminds the Abbot that he is a relative, and that J.'s rejection would be the more painful *ubi caput loci et regiminis particeps nostri sanguinis existit*.]

240

THE POPE PROVIDES OUT OF THE INCOME OF A BENEFICE WITHOUT THE KNOWLEDGE OF THE PATRONS

Folio 20, d. No. 240. A.D. 1304

[This is a striking instance of Papal "provision." The bishop, William of Gainsborough, writes to the Rural Dean of Worcester.]

"WILLIAM DE STANEWEYE, a poor clerk, has shown us in his petition that some time ago Boniface VIII, the Lord Pope, of happy memory, writing to our predecessor officially—*sub dignitatis nomine*—in his letter in proper form ordered that from some ecclesiastical benefice in the gift of the Prior and Convent of Worcester the Bishop should provide for him. And our predecessor, proceeding rightly according to the Apostolic mandate, ordered that the provision should be made from the next benefice that fell vacant in the gift of the Convent. The church of Overbury in this diocese, in their gift, being now vacant in law and in fact, William has humbly requested us to provide for him from the church of Overbury, and induct him to corporal possession and defend him so inducted. We, as bound by obedience to the Apostolic mandate, request a reply from you.

"Since we may expect as a result of the death of him who gave the order, and of the action of the said Convent and of William that fresh complications may arise, and wishing to have full information as to the whole business from the parties themselves, we straitly charge you to cite the said Prior and Convent of Worcester to appear before us or our commissary in person, or a proper representative, on the third legal day—*dies juridicus*—after the feast of the Holy Trinity next occurring, wherever we shall then be in our diocese, to bring forward and prove, as far as rights permit, if they have any canonical reason to urge why in accordance with the Apostolic command and decree so interposed, we are not bound to the said William, the poor clerk, in this matter to provide him from the church of Overbury: and to receive further whatever shall be in accordance with reason.

"Certify us on the day named by your letters patent how you execute this mandate.

"Gloucester, May 12, 1304."

253

THE BISHOP SELECTS A PROMISING SCHOLAR FROM AMONG THE MONKS

Folio 21, d. No. 253. A.D. 1304

"BROTHER W., by Divine permission humble minister of the church of Worcester, to his beloved sons in Christ, the Prior and Convent of the same church, salvation, grace, and blessing.

"Being desirous that, through the study and teaching of sacred literature, both the honour of God and the advance of our church should be augmented, we earnestly require and request your prompt attention, as you are bound to have the same desire as ourselves, that you will not permit our beloved in Christ, brother Ranulph de Catthrop, who, as we have learned, has up to this time made praiseworthy progress both in learned studies—*in scientiali studio*—and in uprightness of character, to be hindered in any way in so fruitful an occupation, but rather that by sending him to a place of study, you should procure, as far as in you lies, that what he has well begun should be even better completed.

"Pray do not oppose our request; and be assured that what we now seek only by words we are prepared when the opportunity comes to support by deeds.

"May you ever be strong in the Lord. Given at Alvechurch, August 20, 1304."

[Ranulph went to Oxford and took his degree as master, and became a lecturer on Scripture in the monastery, and was for a time lent to the monastery of Ramsey.]

258

MANUMISSION OF A SERF IN MINOR ORDERS

Folio 21, d. No. 258. A.D. 1304

[This is a somewhat exceptional manumission by the Bishop, confirmed by the Convent.]

"BROTHER William, by Divine permission Bishop of Worcester, to his beloved son John de Trobemorton, of our diocese, established in minor orders, salvation, grace, and benediction.

"Favourably regarding thy devotion and the laudatory testimony as to thy life, manners and conversation which reaches us from trustworthy men personally acquainted with thee, and also other merits assigned to thee, we grant thee by these presents free leave to minister in the Orders thou hast received, and to be lawfully promoted to all Holy Orders and to a benefice with or without cure of souls; and the right of administering and disposing of all thy chattels and goods, notwithstanding that thou didst draw thy origin from my *nativi*, or those of my predecessors.

"Bredon, June 10, 1304.

"We, the aforesaid Prior and Chapter, recognize that the aforesaid manumission and leave are correctly and canonically given; and holding them to be valid and sound, we confirm them as far as in us lies by affixing the seal of our chapters; on condition, however (*ita tamen*), that our Chapter is not by reason of this instrument burdened for the future."

[That the son of a serf should have the education of a clerk and be qualified for minor orders indicates the existence of schools at hand.]

266

AN ILLEGAL PRESENTATION TO CROPTHORNE FORCED ON THE CONVENT

Folios 22–25. Nos. 266–349. A.D. 1305

[The presentations to benefices test and exhibit the sense of responsibility in a Church for the right use of its revenues; and the *Liber Albus* throws much light on this subject because it frequently gives the correspondence that preceded the presentation. Some of the letters are quite normal, though the rule that only presbyters should be presented is disregarded: but other presentations possess features of interest.

I will give in brief the story of the presentation of Ingelard, keeper of the wardrobe to the Prince of Wales, to the Rectory of Cropthorne. It shows how the prior and convent were practically forced by the Prince of Wales, afterwards Edward II, to make a corrupt and illegal appointment. It is a lengthy and somewhat tangled correspondence.]

On January 1, 1305, the Prince of Wales writes (266) to the Convent to request that they will, as soon as convenient, present his beloved clerk, Ingelard of Warley, to a suitable benefice in their gift; and until they can do so grant him a pension. Ingelard, it must be noted, is not in any orders.

The Prior replies (274) also in French (which is in this correspondence used in the *Liber* for the first time), that, moved by the Prince's prayers, the Convent grants to Ingelard "for the merits as they understand of his life and conversation," a pension of four marks a year. A mark, it may be noted, was then equal in purchasing power to about £10 of our money. In return they beg for the Prince's help in securing the appropriation of the church of Dodderhill for the Convent. The Prince thanks them (300), and asks them to present Ingelard to the next vacant benefice in their gift.

Some months pass ; and on July 8, 1305, the Prince writes (313) and asks definitely for the living of Cropthorne for Ingelard. The Prior naturally replies that it is not vacant. Peter de Pyriton, a man of considerable distinction, who has been brought back from the diocese of Salisbury, is Rector of Cropthorne, and also of Overbury. Nevertheless on July 15, under pressure, the Prior and Convent make a secret presentation of Ingelard to Cropthorne ; and Ingelard swears, " So help me God and the Saints I will never put forward this presentation until Master Peter vacates it, or by your advice it shall be that I put it forward."

It will be interesting to have the oath in its quaint French. " Sy deu me eyde et les seyns ioe ne metterez jammes avant cest presentement eyns qe mistre Perys le lese, ou par vostre conseil seyt qe ioe le avant mette."

The Prior then writes (316) to Peter about the complication. The Prince, he says, is daily urging them to present Ingelard to Cropthorne ; and Ingelard has sworn—and the Prior remarks that this is dangerous—that he did not seek the living until Peter had resigned it. Peter, however, gives no indication of resigning : and on August 12 the Prince writes (325) to the Prior to hurry on the vacancy, and meantime to increase the pension. The Chancellor also, Hugh le Despenser, writes in the same sense.

In 326 we have the Prior's reply, dated August 23. They have tried to persuade Peter to be willing kindly to resign at once—*qe ille le voyle en bone manere resigner hastivement*—and he will not do so. Nevertheless, Peter continues to hold house and income, and refuses to quit. Naturally, the Prince is very angry: he had given orders: the business must not be delayed. Ingelard also writes a letter *maximæ indignationis*. The Prior once more urges Peter to get them out of the difficulty by resigning, but in vain. Peter will not move.

The Prior then writes (328) a somewhat obscure letter to the Prince, in which he appears to beg that the Prince will make it a command; apparently so as to shift the responsibility and throw it on the King: but he adds, in answer to a question whether the living was vacant or no, that the Bishop had stated that he understood that on September 7 the living was vacant before God and the law.

In 330 we have an impatient letter (September 20, 1305) from the Prince, concluding with a threat; in reply to which the Convent raise the pension from four marks to six. A personal interview with Ingelard is arranged, two monks being deputed to go and see him. But on September 29, 1305, Peter resigns (344), as he declares voluntarily—*volens de certis causis exonerari cura Ecclesiæ memoratæ*—claiming his books and crops and hay and all his property in the church, the manse, and elsewhere.

Ingelard is then again on December 7 presented to Cropthorne (349), and we hear no more of him in the *Liber Albus*. Bishop Gainsborough's Register simply records that on September 24, 1306, in the Cathedral, Ingelard of Warley was ordained acolyte and subdeacon on the title of Rector of Cropthorne.

It has been a long story; but it is thoroughly characteristic of the age. Under pressure from the Prince of Wales and the Chancellor, the Convent presents, and the Bishop institutes, a layman to a rectory which is not vacant, and a valued scholar is forced to make way for him.*

The future of Ingelard seems to have been worthy of this beginning. We get glimpses of him from the papal letters, and Rymer's *Fœdera*, and our own Bursar's rolls. Thus we learn that in May 1307 he holds two livings, and the Pope licenses him to hold one more. In March 1308 he holds three livings, and the Pope licenses him to hold two more. In 1309 he visits the monastery with a train of horsemen, and puts the Convent to great expense. In 1312 he is in such serious trouble with the Bishop of Lichfield that the Prince, now Edward II, has to beg the Pope to intercede and get him excused. I have not traced his fortunes further.

Pluralities were not exceptional; but the State was more to blame than the Church. I give one more illustration, not from the *Liber Albus*. At Godfrey Giffard's council at Hartlebury in 1300 the case of Ralph of Hengham, a non-resident pluralist, was brought forward. He had held a canonry in the collegiate church of Warwick for over twenty years; and in 1294 he held no less than fourteen benefices with cure of souls. He had been Chief Justice of the King's Bench from 1274 to 1290, when he was imprisoned and fined for perversion of justice: but in 1300 he was again among the judges who were summoned to Parliament. In 1303 our Prior is corresponding with him (155) as Chief Justice in the Court of Chancery. What was the result of the council at Hartlebury to consider the scandal? It was decided that as Ralph of Hengham was one of the King's Council it was inexpedient to proceed against him.

Other unworthy presentations were forced on our

* There is some confusion in dates which I am unable wholly to resolve.

Prior by the Bishop and by the Pope, and of these I give details in my paper to the Worcestershire Historical Society for the year 1919. A reference to *Papal Letters*, vol. ii, pp. 52, 60, will show what Clement V would sanction. One instance is that he grants a dispensation to a boy of ten to hold two benefices, and when he is fourteen he may hold two more.

THE PRESIDENT OF THE GENERAL CHAPTER URGES THE PRIOR AND CONVENT TO RESTORE THE LECTURESHIP ON THEOLOGY IN THE MONASTERY

Folio 23, d. No. 315. A.D. 1305

" You have been accustomed in your monastery to elect a prudent, fit and learned man, who is able to discharge the office of lector by reading Holy Scripture, and we believe that this has been usually done not only in your church by election, but in all cathedral churches, as expressly decreed by the constitutions of the holy fathers the Roman pontiffs, and we find the custom to be observed in the great majority of them.

" But you in your monastery, as we have learned from the report of trustworthy persons, have now for two years abandoned a practice so sanctioned, to the prejudice of your church, the blackness of your reputation, and the loss of both seculars and regulars. Compensation for things that have been lost does not go far to supply the benefit of restoration, as is not surprising.

" We are desirous, to the utmost of our power, to obviate the malicious and evil reports which have for these reasons spread among people about you, and therefore advise and command you, each and all, to take pains to recall the custom, or rather the solemn and venerable ordinance, by electing some one to read Holy Writ and preach the Divine Word, as in past times had been the continued custom, lest the diocesan be forced to apply his helping hand, and at his coming the secrets of our Order should be revealed, to the exclusion of the visitors of our General Chapter, which we should not wish.

" Be strong in Him who is the true Salvation of all."

Note.—It appears from this letter that the lectures on theology in a monastery were open to secular clerks as well as to the regulars. The anxiety to avoid the intervention of the Bishop is noteworthy.

[This letter was printed by the late Mr. A. F. Leach in his *Early Education in Worcester* from another copy, Worc. Hist. Soc., 1912.]

321

HOW THE KING DEALT WITH AN OUTBREAK OF DISORDER AND ROBBERY

(TRAYLEBASTON)

Folio 25, r. Nos. 321–324. A.D. 1305

[This is summarized in the margin as Straylebaston.]

DUCANGE explains *hoc est trahe baculum : vox Vulgaris apud Anglos*. These special justices were appointed by Edward I in 1304 to deal with gangs of robbers and malefactors. In *Annales de Wigornia*, under the year 1305, we read, " In this year for the first time justices of our lord the King—*qui vocantur Trailbastun* —travelled through England and sat at Worcester. The letters that follow give a glimpse of their proceedings.

A WRIT FROM THE KING (321) TO THE SHERIFF OF WORCESTER

" Edward, etc. Since we have appointed our beloved and faithful William Martyn, Henry Spigurnell, Gilbert de Knovill, Roger de Bellofago, and Thomas de la Hyde as our justices to inquire on oath from soldiers and from other honest and lawful—*legales*—men of your country both within and without the liberties, through whom the truth of things may be best known as to the malefactors and disturbers of our peace, who are perpetrating by day and by night very numerous homicides, plunderings, burnings, men wandering dispersed in your county, and to hear of their felonies and transgressions, and to put an end to them according to the law and custom of our realm, and the ordinance made for this purpose by us and our council, and committed to these five men in our Parliament, we order you that at times and places which they or any four, three or two of them may name to you, you shall collect before them soldiers and other honest and lawful men, in such numbers and of such quality as they require, from whom the truth of these matters may be best inquired and known; and that you shall obey, assist and attend these five, or any four, three, or two of them, as they may direct in our behalf. Produce then this writ. Witnessed by myself, at Westminster, April 6, in the thirty-third year of our reign."

322

How the Justices Obeyed the Order

"W. Martyn, H. Spigurnell, to the beloved Sheriff of Worcester, greeting.

"On the part of our lord the King we order you to assemble before us and our companions at Worcester on the day after the Assumption of the Blessed Mary, twenty-four men, both soldiers and other trusty and lawful men from every hundred of your county, both within and without the liberties, and twenty-four trusty and lawful men from each town that responds with twelve. And similarly twelve trusty and lawful men from each of its towns that responds with six; and from every other town four men, by whom the truth of things may best be inquired and known, for an inquiry into certain affairs touching the King himself. You shall also cause to appear before us at a certain time and place all the coroners of the said county, and similarly all those who have filled the office of coroner since the twenty-fifth year of the King, or their heirs, if they themselves have died, with their rolls and documents concerning the coroner's business, to certify us on certain matters which specially touch our said lord the King. And you yourself shall be present in your own person as you wish to escape blame in doing all that we shall order in the name of our lord the King.

"Bring with you then the original brief of our lord the King which came to you from him, and also this brief.

"Given at Winchester on Wednesday after the feast of St. James the Apostle (July 29)."

323

Memorandum of their Doings

The aforesaid justices came for the first time to Worcester on the day after the Assumption of St. Mary the Virgin, A.D. 1305, and in 33 Ed. I, and sat there on the first occasion for six days. W. Martyn and G. Knovill stayed at the priory. Three men only were hanged, nearly nine score were proclaimed—*fuerunt in exigendis*. Afterwards they sat at Hereford and Leominster.

324

An Accident (*Casus*)

"They came again to Worcester on the Vigil of the Nativity of the Blessed Mary, and sat four days. Three men were hanged, and the third of them when he was taken down from the gallows to the cemetery moved himself and retained some life, and through one night he lived at St. Wulstan's tomb."

345

A MEMORANDUM OF A DEBT

Folio 25, d. No. 345. A.D. 1305

"Memorandum that on November 2 we are bound to Richard de la Lynde in £62, to be paid him at the feast of Pentecost and in the quinzaine* of St. Michael in the thirty-fourth year. And the total sum of our whole debt to him on the day after All Saints is £304 6s. 8d.

"33 Ed. I."

* Quinzaine is equivalent to two octaves.

357

THE BISHOP RETURNING FROM FRANCE BEGS FOR THE GIFT OF A HORSE

Folio 26, d. No. 357. A.D. 1306

" To the reverend father in Christ William, by the grace of God Lord Bishop of Worcester, brother John, the humble Prior of the same place, due obedience and reverence in all things with honour.

" We have understood from your holiness's letters that you have happily passed through the dangers of the roads and have returned safe to your native soil. We offer you many congratulations and return our special thanks to the Most High for so great a blessing.

" Moreover, you have written that you are in need of a horse, with which you hope to be supplied by us. Appreciating therefore the confidence which you have in us, we order a horse to be placed at your disposal, such as we possess, grieving that it is so poor and thin, for your use. Did our power equal our good-will we would gladly have sent you one more serviceable.

" May your reverend lordship have health and strength long to rule and defend our church."

Note.—In the margin it is noted that the horse, *modicus et exilis*, was called Hoel.

formally appoint two of their number as proctors, with full power to represent the Convent in all courts, to object to "brother John called Thoky, who has been elected, as is said, Abbot of St. Peter's, Gloucester, and to bring forward against him and the persons who elect him the sentence of greater excommunication."

The new Abbot was John Thoky, the sub-Prior. On what grounds he was so warmly objected to by our Prior and Convent, or what business they had to interfere, it is not told.

The next letter (363) is from John himself to inform our Prior that after his benediction and confirmation he proposes to proceed to his installation on June 29, and affectionately supplicates, that "in order to bring to a laudable end the proceedings of that day to their mutual consolation and honour, he will deign to vouchsafe his venerable presence."

An abstract only of the reply is given in 364. It is to the effect that unless an order from the King, or very pressing business of the house prevents him, he will be present. It is summarized in the margin as "An excuse," so we may assume, I think, that the Prior found pressing business at home.

A reconciliation seems to have been effected; for next year, in 1307, we read in 378 that our Prior writes to ask a special favour on the ground of the Abbot's "friendship and goodwill to us and our monastery." The favour consists in showing grace and favour, consistent with justice, towards Worcester in a lawsuit against the monastery which the Pope has referred to him to decide.

The transitions from war to friendship and back again come as suddenly as slides in a magic lantern. For details of the suit with the Abbot of Gloucester, see *Sede Vacante Register* (Worc. Hist. Soc.), p. 120.

There is a vacancy in the See, from the death of Bishop Gainsborough: our Prior, with an eye to fees, claims the right to visit the abbey of Gloucester: and with due notice presents himself on the Vigil of Palm Sunday at the gates of the abbey, and demands entrance. It is refused by two proctors for the abbey standing outside. He hands them a note by which he excommunicates abbot, prior, sub-prior, cellerar, precentor, hostiler, kitchener, infirmarer, and almoner; and sends it to the Dean of Gloucester, who causes it to be published in every church in the city for the next three Sundays. But now the official of the Archbishop intervenes, and inhibits our Prior: the Abbot has shown (1) that it is not decided that the Prior has any right of visitation; (2) that it is only two years since the Bishop visited it; (3) that it is notorious that the new Bishop, Walter Reynolds, has been appointed. So, finally, it is all referred to the Archbishop, and the storm settles down.

But on the next vacancy it all breaks out again.

Again our Prior demands the right to visit the abbey, *sede vacante*: again the gates are closed: and again he excommunicates Abbot and obedientiaries, and writes plaintively to the new Bishop, Walter de Maidstone (614, 616) on his appointment, imploring him not to release the excommunication and sequestration he has imposed; and, further, he complains, that though excommunicated "they all persevere, and have for forty days persevered with hardened mind, to the peril of their souls, wickedly contemning the keys of the church." He, therefore, earnestly requests the Bishop to write to the King to order their arrest, "according to the laudable custom of the realm; lest such temerity, going unpunished, give to others an occasion for crime." He writes a similar letter to the Archbishop (617).

The Bishop assures the Prior that not only against the Abbot of Gloucester, but against all others who injure or molest them or their monastery, he will support them.

They settle down, however, into most amicable relations, all these fireworks and thunder notwithstanding. The most novel and interesting event in the relations of the two convents is yet to be told. It is the story of the sending of an intolerably disagreeable monk of Worcester, Simon of Defford, to be reformed, if possible, in the monastery of Gloucester. This story must be told in full. It is contained in documents 743, 744, dated August 1317: and closes the correspondence of our Prior, John de Wyke. He was ill in September, and died on October 5 of that year.

" To the reverend father in the Lord, by the grace of God the Lord Abbot of St. Peter's, Gloucester, brother John, the humble Prior of the cathedral church of Worcester, and the chapter of the same place, greeting and sincere charity in the Lord.

" In the halls of the house of God it becomes and behoves those who serve together in the dress of our holy religion to walk in harmony, and to preserve in all things the bond of peace. But in our community—*collegium*—there is a certain brother who, by his violent language, has greatly disturbed the peace and the quiet intercourse of the brethren. We have borne with it for many days, carrying this burden on our weary shoulders, in the hope of some amendment to come, of which, however, we see no signs. Many circumstances therefore, indeed urgent necessity, and the fear that such rebellion and unreasonableness may, if unpunished, set to others a pernicious example, and give them audacity in disobedience, compel us to think of some remedy.

"When, therefore, recently we were carefully considering how to correct the excesses of our brother, and restore quiet in our community, there came among other things to our recollection that laudable statute, which in our last General Chapter, held at Northampton, was drawn up almost precisely for chastising this sort of disturber of peace. The statute referred to was, therefore, read aloud in our chapter, and a public inquiry was then made at the meeting as to the intolerable behaviour of the said brother; and it was found by the larger and saner part of the chapter, indeed by the whole convent, that the brother we have indicated was a perturber of peace, disturbing our customary quiet. We, therefore, by common consent decreed that this state of things must be put an end to.

"We hoped that our brother could be forced to penitence and amendment in your monastery more effectively and in accordance with the rule than anywhere else; and, therefore, we sent our brother and fellow-monk, Master John de Harley, to you with our letters of credence; and he in our name, by word of mouth, pleaded with your fatherly heart that you would admit the said brother for a time to perform his penance in your monastery, for his amendment and our quiet, and also for the honour of our Order. To this request, as we have learned from the tenor of your letters, you have courteously consented.

"For this consent, in addition to the reward which you will receive in the sight of God for your conspicuous obedience in this matter to the presidents and prelates of our Order and to their statutes, we also convey to you our thanks, to be expressed in manifold actions.

"After being entertained among you as a guest for

one night in any way you think best, let him on the morrow have a bed assigned him in some part of your common dormitory; and after that let him be admitted in the chapter house in presence of all. Let him then be conducted outside, and, while the chapter meeting goes on, let him have a fixed place assigned him in your cloisters apart from the novices; and meantime let the brethren be informed of the reason of his coming. Thenceforward let him take his place in the convent as a novice not professed, and be placed last but one among the younger priests —*sacerdotes*—on the left side of the choir. When he has been instructed by some guardian as to your mode of chanting and reading in the church, let him take his share, as you may arrange, in the work of Divine service, along with the rest of the juniors. Then, if it should seem to you expedient, let him be placed in order for everything except Masses; we do not intend to impose on him the celebration of the solemnity of the Mass until he has established peace with his neighbours and himself. In other matters let him do whatever he is asked to do.

"But of outside service let him omit nothing; he should dine only in the refectory; and on no account let him drink wine. Let him sleep in the dormitory; not go outside the cloister; and nowhere, except in the presence of some guardian of the Order, hold conversation with any one, whether a stranger or known to you. Let secret confabulations in the same way be forbidden; it will not be expedient, in a place of silence and quiet, to hear his noisy lips and braggart tongue.

"Be good enough, if you please, when you see the right moment, to let us know concerning any signs of penitence and improvement in him, as soon as they seem to be established, and how he behaves in obeying the rules laid down; and we will certainly arrange for his further treatment by lightening, or if need be increasing, his burden, as his conduct may require.

"If during the time he is with you he should be ill, treat him in all respects as you would treat one of similar position in your own community—*familia.* It only remains to say that as to his expenses for the whole time of his sojourn with you we will fully satisfy you whenever you wish, according to the terms of the statute referred to.

"May the Most High for ever guard your kind Paternity."

The letter indicates that the matter had been settled previously, by a visit from one of the Worcester monks; and the consent of the Abbot had been given in the letter that follows, addressed by him to the Prior.

"The beloved in Christ, John de Harley, your fellow-monk, came to us and showed us your friendly letter of credence, and afterwards, by word of mouth, in your name, explained to us that a certain member of your college, a brother and fellow-monk, was showing himself so troublesome that for the welfare and honour of our common religion it seemed to you expedient that he should be placed for a time among us in our monastery; and he earnestly entreated us to meet your wish in this matter. We desire you, as a friend, to know that when the brother comes to us with your letters we will admit and welcome him; and guided by the contents of those letters, and in accordance with the Rule of St. Benedict, and the honour of our Order, we will secure, so far as lies in our power, that he is rightly treated during the time that he is with us: and about his conduct and degree of penitence we will send you information as soon as anything seems to us to be certain.

"May your Reverence long have honour and strength in Christ.

"Given at Gloucester on the day of St. Bartholomew the Apostle, August 24, 1317."

Two months later, on October 29 in the same year 1317, Simon is required to return to Worcester to give his vote at the election of the new prior; but he returns to Gloucester.

How does this interesting experiment turn out? As far as I have yet read the *Liber Albus* it was an entire success. On December 17 of the same year the new Prior of Worcester, Wulstan de Bransford, writes (768) to the Abbot of Gloucester that as they hear that now for a long time Simon has behaved in a praiseworthy manner they wish to recall him: and with warm expressions of their thanks they send forty shillings in payment.

The Abbot in 769 replies in the most courteous way that Simon has behaved so devoutly and obediently, that they are much bound to him. He begs that he may be allowed to return the money, and assures the Prior that Simon's honourable return to Gloucester would give them very great pleasure—*quod ipsius ad nos regressus honestus nobis ingens gaudium erit allaturus*.

Note.—From 1011 it appears that John de Waleys, a Worcester monk, was similarly sent to Abergavenny under discipline.

365

A CITATION FOR THE COLLECTION OF FIRST-FRUITS AND OTHER CHARGES

Folio 26, d. Nos. 365, 366. A.D. 1306

[The following document is of considerable historical interest. It is the citation issued to a deanery by the Prior, acting as commissary for William Testa, Archdeacon of Arenns (in the Pyrenees) in the church of Comminges, and for William Gerald de Sora, Canon of Rouen, chaplains of the Pope, and principal collectors of first-fruits for Pope Clement V. It is addressed to the Dean of Campden.]

"BROTHER John, the humble Prior of the cathedral church of Worcester, appointed commissary in the city and diocese of Worcester of the men of religion, Masters William Testa, Archdeacon of Arenns in the Church *Convenarum*, and of William Gerald de Sora, Canon of Rouen, chaplains of the Lord Pope, and principal collectors of the fruits of the first year of ecclesiastical benefices now vacant and which shall chance to be vacant for the year, which our most holy father Pope Clement, for certain lawful reasons reserves for himself in England, Wales, Scotland, and Ireland for the Apostolic See—to the man of discretion, the Dean of Campden, greeting in our Saviour.

"By the Apostolic authority committed to me, in this matter, in virtue of the obedience you are bound to render to the Apostolic See, we strictly enjoin and command you to cite or cause to be cited peremptorily all rectors and vicars, and all the religious of whatever Order, exempt and non-exempt, and all the Hospitallers, Templars, and all others of whatever pre-eminence, rank, and condition they are, who are known to hold ecclesiastical benefices within the boundaries or limits of your deanery, and specially all and each of those who since the kalends of February last past have received benefices, that they appear before us or before Thomas de Weston, our colleague in this matter, or his or our deputy in the church of the Blessed Mary of Campden, on the first legal day after the feast of St. Kenelm, King and martyr, to hear the Apostolic mandate in this matter; and those who are beneficed since the last-named kalends are to give full replies as to the fruits that they have received after the time of their institution, and also as to the fruits which they may receive, either personally or by well-informed proctors.

"You are to request, induce and exhort them to send in all that has been overlooked, and also to enjoin them that no one who has been beneficed since the said last kalends shall in any way by alienating, dividing or dispersing any of the fruits derived from his benefices interfere for the future, until he has some other orders from us or our superiors aforesaid.

"You are also to cite, or cause to be cited, by the authority of the same William Testa, nuncio of our lord the Pope, and promoter and commissary of the affairs of the Holy Land, all and each of the rectors and vicars residing in your deanery, and in other churches where the rectors do not reside the parish chaplains, and from every parish four trustworthy men by whose means the truth can best be ascertained, that at the said time and place they are to appear before us or our deputy, on the matter of legacies not clearly left—*indistincte relictis*—and of pecuniary fines in aid of the Holy Land, promised or pledged in contracts in any way; and also of all payments which are in any way whatever, for any reason or cause, owing on these accounts to the Roman Church, from wills and vows, or from redemption of vows, whether of *crucesignati* (for the crusades), or of others in aid of the Holy Land; and they are to speak pure and unmixed truth, and to act further as shall be just and right.

"What you do in this business you are to certify me by your letters in full detail.

"Given at Worcester."

The commission was received through Master Thomas de Weston, V. Ides (11th) of July, A.D. 1306.

366

Interrogatoria

"In the first place let inquiry be made where benefices were in law and in fact vacant from February 1, and which are vacant at present.

"Item, what persons have accepted the said benefices.

"Item, let inquiry be made as to the value of the first-fruits of the benefices.

"Item, who received those first-fruits.

"Item, about legacies and remainders not clearly left, who received them, and who were executors of the said wills, and into whose hands the goods of the deceased passed.

"Item, let inquiry be made concerning pecuniary fines in aid of the Holy Land, promised, pledged, and to be pledged in any contracts, and who promised those fines.

"Item, what are the names of the *crucesignatorum testā vel ab intestato decedentium.*

"Item, let inquiry be made concerning the names of those who in those parts from any reason or cause are in any way bound in debt to the Roman Church from wills, vows or redemption of vows, whether *cruce-*

signati or others, in any form of subsidy to the Holy Land.

" Also let inquiry be made as to St. Peter's pence in every parish, if they are full, and in what manner, for what amount how far they are bound . . . [erasions here] . . . are collected and paid in the usual way ; and if not who have them in each parish, and in whose hands the said pence remain to be paid."

Accordingly in 370 we have a mandate sent to the Prior by the Bishop ordering him to give to the executors of Godfrey Giffard all the property they held under the will of the late Bishop, including sums pledged to the Holy Land ; and in 372 we have the receipt of the executors.

388

QUEEN MARGARET WRITES TO THE PRIOR AND CONVENT ON THE DEATH OF KING EDWARD I

Folio 28, d. No. 388. A.D. 1307

"MARGARET, by the Grace of God Queen of England, Lady of Ireland, and Duchess of Aquitaine, to our beloved in God, the Prior and Convent of Worcester, salvation in our Saviour.

"Since cruel death, which none can escape, has taken from us our very dear lord the King, and removed him from this world, to the heavy loss of ourselves and of all Christendom, as it seems to us; and sorrow and pain have therefore grievously wounded our hearts, we pray you, with all the earnestness in our power, that having regard to the goodwill which our said lord had towards you and your church in his time, you will have his soul specially commended to God in all your holy services—*vueillez avoir l'alme de li especiaument recomendie entre totes vos seyntes œuvres*—and pray devoutly for him to God, that by His grace, and for the great faith he had during his life He will show him true mercy, and deign to receive him among His chosen. We hope that this will please God; and we and our children will be henceforward bound to you for this reason.

"What you are pleased to do in the matter above spoken of kindly write in your letter to us by the bearer of these presents, for the love you bear towards the soul of our said lord, and towards us.

"May our Lord guard you.

"Given at Barnwell, near Cambridge, on August 2."

[The King died at Burgh-on-the-Sand, near Carlisle, July 7, 1307; but his death was for a time not made widely known.]

389

THE REPLY OF THE PRIOR AND CONVENT

Folio 28, d. No. 389. A.D. 1307

"To the most honourable and mighty Lady, their lady Margaret, by the grace of God Queen of England, Lady of Ireland, and Duchess of Aquitaine, her humble and devoted Prior and Convent of Worcester; salvation, with all that they are or can offer of reverence and honour.

"For that which, most dear Lady, you have told us by your letter, that our lord the King is commended to God, and withdrawn from this world, we are much pained and made sorrowful at heart. May God of His pity show him true mercy—*que Dieu par sa pité Lui face veoray merci.*

"You wish that we should specially commend his soul to God in our services and prayers, and that we should reply in our letter, by the bearer of yours, what it shall please us to do in the matter above named. We desire you to know, most dear Lady, that with entire goodwill we will sing specially for the soul of our said lord fifteen hundred Masses, and that every day he shall be a sharer in all our holy services and our good prayers. We will enter his name in our martyrology, and devoutly keep his anniversary for the future, as our lord and as a brother of our chapter. We are much bound to him by the goodwill which in his time he showed to us and to our church, and for the great bounty and privileges which he then often conferred on us, and by your requests, which, most dear Lady, are to us commands, you lay upon us as your wishes.

"May God ever preserve and guard you, and give you long life and health.

"Given at Worcester, the 9th day of August."

399

ST. AUGUSTINE'S CANTERBURY INVITES A WORCESTER MONK TO BE THEIR LECTURER IN SCRIPTURE

Folio 30, r. Nos. 399, 400, 397. A.D. 1308

[Lecturers fully qualified by a University degree as *sacræ paginæ professores* were rare; one of the Worcester monks, John de St. German, who had been elected by the monks as their bishop, on the death of Godfrey Giffard, but was refused by the Pope, was a well-known scholar.]

"THOMAS, etc., Minister of St. Augustine's Monastery, Canterbury, to the Prior and Convent of Worcester.

"The sincere charity which ought specially to exist among the religious, and those bound together by the chain of fraternal love, gives an innate call that brothers should with kind hearts share with brothers in things which are required for their pious duties towards God. We also, fully relying on the benevolence of your holy congregation, approach you in our business with all the more confidence, as we hope without doubt for the assent to our request which we desire.

"Since many of our brethren, anxious to make progress, greatly desire to devote themselves to the study of scholastic discipline, while we are still unable to provide ourselves with a lecturer, we beg for one of your brethren, one whom with sincere affection we love in the Lord, viz. that man of discretion, John Germeyn, whose soundness in learning and character we have heard warmly commended, and whose coming to us we have for these reasons long desired. We have, therefore, resolved to entreat your beloved brother in the very bowels of charity, that with his and your unanimous goodwill, you will deign graciously to grant that he may at least for a time by your licence be put in charge of the instruction of our brethren in Holy Scripture.

"May these our prayers for him thus humbly offered, be so accepted, we beg, in your holiness's heart, that your kindness may entrust to our porter a gracious reply on this matter to be carried back to us."

400

The Abbot of St. Augustine's Canterbury writes to him as follows:

"To the man of religion and discreet brother and most dear friend in Christ, brother John Germeyn, monk of the church of Worcester, Thomas, by Divine permission Abbot of the monastery of St. Augustine at Canterbury, health and brotherly love in the Lord.

"Since our brethren one and all ardently desire your bodily presence, in order that they may be instructed by you in Holy Scripture; and since we and our Convent have written to your Prior and Convent to obtain your liberty to accept, devoutly in the Lord we beg your fraternity that, weighing our affection for you, you would be pleased, as far as in you lies, graciously to grant our request, to wit, that if, as we hope, you assent to our desires, that you should be with us, if possible soon after this next feast of St. John the Baptist.

"Concerning all which things you will be good enough to inform us by letter through the bearer of this.

"May your fraternity fare well in Our Lord Jesus Christ and the glorious Virgin.

"Given at Canterbury on April 20, 1308. To be

delivered to brother John Germeyn, monk of the church of Worcester."

397

The Prior replies to the Abbot as follows :

" Since it is a pious deed, and consonant with charity gladly to assent to the just petitions of friends, and to grant those which effect the wishes of such as desire to promote the common advantage and honour of all in the Church of God, we agree gladly to your pious supplication for the consent of our brethren for the sake of increasing for the future our mutual affection ; and we grant to our beloved in Christ, our brother and fellow-monk, John de St. German, a special licence to go to you whenever you wish, to give instruction in Holy Scripture, and the refreshment of the Word of God, until we shall think it right to recall him.

" Should there be any matters which can be forwarded by us for you or yours, we shall not be found wanting in diligent care for you or affection.

" May your holy congregation and devotion in Christ long continue."

403

PROVISION MADE FOR A VICAR

Folio 30, d. No. 403. A.D. 1304

[The appropriation of benefices to the use of monasteries became at this time very common: and provision was not always made for the cure of souls in the parish.]

"To all members of holy Mother Church to whose knowledge this writing may come, brother William (Gainsborough), by Divine permission Bishop of Worcester, everlasting salvation in the Lord.

"We make it known by these presents to all of you —*universitas vestra*—that recently we found that the church of Child's Wickham in our diocese, which under the title of appropriation had been applied to the personal needs of the men of religion, the Abbot and Convent of Bordesley of the Cistercian Order, by the Lord Godfrey of good memory our predecessor, was destitute of the solace of a vicar; and that no sufficient provision for the support of a vicar had been arranged by our predecessor or by any one else, or was in any way existing. We being anxious to keep in view that the said parish should suffer no loss; and that the souls of its parishioners should be provided for; anxious also to obey canonical laws as we are bound to do; having first obtained the written and explicit submission of brother J. the Abbot, and of the Convent of the said place, sealed by their seal and now in our custody, do make order henceforth that a vicar shall be appointed in that church with whom will rest the cure of souls, and who shall reside there continually; and for his support in the aforesaid church of Wykewane we make order as follows:

"We, brother Walter, by Divine permission Bishop of Worcester, after inquiry made in accordance with our mandate by trustworthy men, rectors, vicars, chaplains, and laity in sufficient numbers, men who were likely to have the fullest knowledge of the true value of all sources of income, sworn and straitly charged to report the true value of all the income of the said church and of every particular of its income, such as it produces in ordinary years, do hereby order, decree, appoint, and will that the support or suitable sustentation for the perpetual vicar whose duty it is to serve the said church shall consist of the payments written below.

"To wit, of a certain area—*area*—in the township of Wykewane, in which is situated a certain house called the priest's house, with all the area adjacent to it; and of a certain garden defined on the western side of the rectory manse by hedges and ditches, as are now included, lying between the manse on one side and the pool of the watermill—*molendinum aquaticum*—on the other, to be satisfactorily built by the Abbot and Convent before St. John Baptist's Day next occurring; and of tithes, and other payments to the said church written below.

"That is to say, of the tithe of wool, milk, calves, young pigs, geese, eggs, honey and bees, gardens, curtilages, land dug with spade, doves, mills of every kind, flax, hemp.

"Also of all mortuary fees save only those which have to be paid in live animals.

"Also of offerings of all kinds at the altar, living creatures, trentals, requisitions for the departed, and in general of all small tithes and contributions to the altar by whatever name either now or at a later time they may be described.

"Also of the tenth of meadow land, which tenth has hitherto been usually paid in money.

"Also of one quarter of wheat, and of one quarter of barley, pure and clean grain, to be received from the grange of the Abbot and Convent in the town of Wykewane every year in future on St. Martin's Day in the winter.

"We also ordain and decree that the said Abbot and Convent and their successors for ever, shall pay to the vicar for the time being of the aforesaid church of Wykewane sixty shillings sterling, at the times named below—viz., on the feast of the Purification of the glorious Virgin, twenty shillings; on the feast of the Lord's Annunciation—*Annunciationis dominicæ*—twenty shillings; and on the feast of the Holy Trinity, twenty shillings.

"We further order and decree that the said Abbot and Convent shall repair, rebuild, or re-roof the chancel, whenever it shall be necessary, and shall for the future provide sufficient books in the same.

"We further order and decree that the vicar for the time being shall entertain in future the arch-deacon of the place, and besides his due entertainment—*procuratio*—shall pay him annually half a mark sterling, on the feast of the Purification of the glorious Virgin; and that he shall be bound to find linen, vestments, and other ornaments necessary for Divine service in the chancel, and also to provide a competent clerk.

"We also ordain that both the said Abbot and Convent and the said vicar and their successors shall always acknowledge extraordinary claims from time to time, and bear their share, to be divided as in future may be decided.

"To this ruling we hereby add that the arch-deacons of the place and their officials for the time being shall, notwithstanding any privilege whatever obtained or to be obtained from the said Abbot and Convent and their successors, possess the free power to correct, punish, and otherwise exercise archidiaconal powers, as they have been accustomed to exercise them in their own time and that of their predecessors, over the transgressions and sins of the parishioners of the said church, and also of the ministers and servants of the said Abbot and Convent, if committed in the parish itself, and those of all others of whatever state and condition, who have been guilty in the parish or in the rectory manse.

"That this our ruling may have its due result in every detail, and not be exposed to blame in the future, we ordain that we, and the archdeacon of the place, and our successors, and our officials, shall possess the power, without troublesome judicial proceedings, or any form of law, or any warning given, of compelling, when occasion requires, the said Abbot and Convent and their successors to observe all the foregoing, if in any respect, which may God forbid, they wish to infringe our ruling; and to satisfy in the matter of losses or any interests those who may be interested in this matter, by sentences of suspension, excommunication, and interdict, or any other ecclesiastical censure, and by the sequestration of all their property, wherever found, whether in the parish itself or elsewhere in the diocese.

"We reserve for ourselves and our successors four marks sterling as procuration, from the income of the said Abbot and Convent in the said church, to be paid every year in future, to those who are appointed by us or our successors to visit the church, under penalties notified above.

"We reserve also for ourselves and our cathedral

church of Worcester the dignity in all matters due to the Bishop and the cathedral, and that of the archdeacon for the time being.

"Given at Alvechurch, the 3rd of the Ides of January, A.D. 1303, in the second year of our consecration."

[Alvechurch, Jan. 11, 1304.]

411

THE CORRODIES GRANTED TO RICHARD DE LA LYNDE AND OTHERS

Folio 31, d. No. 411. A.D. 1308

[A corrody is an allowance made by the Convent to some one for life in return for some benefit conferred, or by the order of the King, or in return for some payment made in cash. They were granted to people of various classes; to men of importance and wealth, like Richard de la Lynde; to old clergy; to their weirman and other old servants. The grant usually included a room, and a defined allowance of food and drink, and very often an allowance for a servant and a horse.

Richard de la Lynde was a rich man who had lent large sums to the Prior. The corrody granted to him is on a more liberal scale, and is more detailed than I have yet met with. It was given in 1308, and is contained in document 411.]

"THE Convent grants to Richard de la Lynde, clerk, for as long as he lives, a room in the priory under the painted chamber, with sufficient straw and firewood to be used when necessary in the fireplace; six pounds of candles of Paris tallow; and 20 shillings a year of lawful money to be paid by the cellerar at Michaelmas.

"Every day of his life he will have one monk's loaf, one white loaf of the old weight, one larger servant's loaf for his attendant; two flagons [= gallons] of superior beer, and one of servant's beer, his attendant having free entry to the *celarium* to fetch it. Every day he will have pottage in quantity and quality the same as a monk; and he will receive from the kitchen one dish of meat as a monk does, either cooked or raw as he prefers. For supper he will receive at the hatch of the misericordia the allowance of two monks.

"On fish days, and on days when copes and albs

are worn (i.e. third and fourth grades of feasts), he will have the same share as a monk of the dish provided by the kitchener or one of our obedientiaries. His attendant will on these days have what is given to the Prior's head-servants.

"He will have a stable, near his room, with three cartloads of hay delivered by us in hay-time at his stable, or he may take enough for one horse in our manor of Herdwick, and ten quarters of oats, either every evening—*noctatim*—or if he prefers, in three equal portions at Michaelmas, the Purification, and Pentecost; also sixteen horseshoes and nails every year of his life."

There are some interesting details in the corrody given (in 654) to Walter Alexander, late Rector of Tibberton, in 1315. He and his boy "are to have daily a monk's loaf and a servant's loaf of the same size, one gallon of best and one of second beer. On flesh days a monk's dish of meat and a monk's pittance. On fish days in Lent four herrings, and of rice as much as a monk. During Advent, if he abstains from meat, as much fish as in Lent. After Easter, on fish days a monk's dish and five eggs."

These permanent guests of a monastery formed an element in the life of the monks that is perhaps not generally realized.

One more may be mentioned: a corrody granted to Henry de Hampton, as a resident medical officer. It is in document 891 of the year 1320. It runs thus: "Be it known to all that we have granted to our beloved in Christ, Master Henry de Hampton, our clerk, for bestowing on us and our brethren for the future his advice, aid and service in the art and practice of medicine, one monk's loaf, one gallon of best beer, and from the kitchen both on meat and fish days a portion such as is served to a monk in the infirmary."

Here is another variety of corrody, in 965:

"The Prior and Convent grant to Godfrey Holyne and Margaret, his wife, half a quarter of wheat every fourth week, six and a half quarters in all. Also at Michaelmas half a quarter of oats and a quarter and a half of barley. Also on Ash Wednesday two hundred red herrings—*alecia rubra*—two salted salmon, and two congers; or if they preferred it, five shillings and four pence."

In 940 a corrody for life is granted to William of Cirencester, chaplain, who pledges himself that as long as he lives and is able he will celebrate Mass daily in such manner and for such persons as the Prior and Convent shall direct.

The *Liber Albus* contains a lengthy correspondence (fifty-one letters) between Edward II, Queen Isabella, and the Prior as to the demand for a corrody for Alicia Conan, a lady-in-waiting on the Queen. The dispute was finally settled at law, in favour of the Prior. This forms the subject of a separate paper in the *Worcester Historical Society Transactions for* 1917.

421

THE MYSTERY OF A LOST MITRE

Folio 32, r. No. 421. A.D. 1322

On August 23, 1308, Bishop Walter Reynolds, soon after his appointment, wrote to the Prior (421): "Since among the vestments you have sent us we do not find a mitre suitable for us, we beg you to send that which you hold in your keeping as a legacy from our predecessor the Lord Godfrey. Please to send it by one of your people, and that with speed, in order that any repairs which may be needed for our use may be made in good time."

On February 26, 1319, Bishop Cobham writes (860) to the Prior that after urgent and reiterated requests the Archbishop, Walter Reynolds, has sent him a noble and beautiful mitre for the Bishop of the diocese, to replace that which the Prior sent him, said to have formerly been Godfrey Giffard's, of far less value. He desires to have a receipt within a month. The Bishop asks the Prior to send by some messenger a letter of receipt duly signed as soon as possible "lest we be blamed for your defect." He encloses a copy of his own receipt of the mitre.

But the Prior is suspicious. He writes (861) that though this sort of handing over and receiving seems on the face of it to be fair and sound, yet when the circumstances are considered, they "cannot, on conscientious grounds—*obstante consciencia*—send him the letter of receipt, without ruinous peril to your cathedral and ours, until the Church is secured against loss, and the danger is past. On this ground, not from unwillingness, but because we cannot do otherwise, deign to excuse us."

More than three years pass; and then on August 30, 1322, Archbishop Walter Reynolds writes to the Prior that "long ago, when Bishop of Worcester, we received from you a certain old-fashioned mitre—*mitram antiquatam*—for our use, and gave you our formal obligatory letter promising to restore it. But after making it far more valuable by gold and gems and precious stones, at great expense, we caused it to be handed over—*liberari*—to our brother the Lord Bishop of Worcester for his use, at his urgent request; the condition being added that within a specified time, long since elapsed, he should return us this obligatory letter; which hitherto he has not done. Since the said mitre, so improved by us, is, as we have understood, now in your possession, we beg that you will be good enough to send back our bond, retaining the mitre. To this release we are entitled from the fact that the mitre has passed into your hands. Kindly inform us what you decide to do."

This seems a most reasonable request.

The Prior acknowledges this letter dated August 30 as received *die commemorationis animarum*, which is November 2. He tells the Archbishop that "the Bishop has refused to hand back the mitre, though we have made diligent demand for it. He has again and again replied that it is in our church: although we have not seen it, nor touched it, nor have been able to get at it. By this defence he wishes to excuse himself and throw the blame on us. We beg you, therefore, to hold us excused from indemnifying you, and beg you to provide some other remedy for our church."

But where is the precious mitre?

429

THE MUNIMENTS OF LANTHONY

Folio 33, r. Nos. 429–431. A.D. 1308

THERE is interesting correspondence on this subject which can only be given in much abridged form.

The Prior of Lanthony-juxta-Gloucester asks the Prior and Convent of Worcester to confirm a copy made in one roll of all their muniments, but beg to be excused from sending the originals owing to the dangers of the roads. The Prior of Worcester replies that the originals must be sent with the copy, and that when they have been examined the copy shall be confirmed. They are sent, and a copy of them is made in our *Liber* filling four pages, giving details of gifts from A.D. 1137 to 1278. The monastery was moved from Monmouthshire to Lanthony in 1136. (See *Monasticon*, new edition, vi, 127 ff., in which the foundation charter of Milo and other charters are given.) The confirmation by the Prior and Convent—*ex certa scientia*—is dated August 18, 1308.

435

THE ADMISSION OF A BROTHER INTO THE SPIRITUAL FRATERNITY

Folio 35, d. No. 435. A.D. 1309

[Convents admitted into their spiritual fraternity some men and women also, who had conferred special benefits on their community. The noble and loving spirit of this fraternity is shown in this letter, No. 409, addressed by the Prior in 1309 to a tried friend of the Convent. We have seen that Edward I was such a brother.]

" BROTHER John, the humble Prior of the cathedral church of Worcester, with the Convent of the same place, prays for his beloved son in Christ, Master John of Bitterley, clerk, that he may have health, and after this life may attain the peace of the faithful.

" Gratitude compels us to confer special honour on those whose kindness to our monastery has been long experienced. Considering, therefore, your brotherly and fruitful and faithful diligence, though you already share in the blessings of our services, Masses, fastings, vigils, prayers, discipline, almsgiving, and in all other works of piety which by God's permission we are allowed to perform, we further desire now to offer to you by this letter that, when your death shall be announced to us or our successors, some priest and professed monk of the church of Worcester shall be bound to celebrate a trental (*tricennale*, or thirty Masses) for you; and the rest of the professed shall sing ten psalters, as for one of our brother-monks when he goes the way of all flesh. We have, therefore, ordered that your name shall be inscribed in our martyrology, to be for ever mentioned on the anniversary of your death; and to ensure the perpetuity of these celebrations we provide 10 shillings as an annual charge on the pittances to be paid to the Convent.

"Signed and sealed in the chapter house on the 7th of the Ides of March, 1308."

John of Bitterley was a clerk under Godfrey Giffard, and acted as his proctor in the Court of Rome.*

Among others who were thus about this time admitted to the fraternity were Michael de Berham, the Bishop of Hereford, the Earl of Lancaster, and John de Lacy, Margaret his wife, Johanna their daughter, and the ladies Alicia and Matilda de Lacy, being nuns.

One regrets to read (in 606) that the Prior and Convent also in the year 1313, with expressions of warm gratitude and admiration, admitted to the same fraternity their late bishop, Walter Reynolds. He was unworthy of the honour.

* In 1324 the Prior and Convent assign him one of the best rooms in the monastery, and support for life for himself and two servants, in return for a moderate payment.

446

PAPAL PROVISIONS OF BENEFICE FOR A BOY

Folio 37, r, *et seq.* Nos. 446–452. A.D. 1309

THESE lengthy documents cannot be given in full, but they are of much interest.

No. 446 is summarized in the margin as "The Process of the provisorial business in the case of John Boter, clerk, brought against the Prior and Convent of Wormeley, executor of the said affair."

The Prior of Wormeley, in the diocese of Hereford, informed the Prior of Worcester that he has received and has to execute a Bull from Pope Clement V. In this Bull it is stated that "in order to encourage John Boter's devotion to the Roman Church, and at the request of the noble Hugo de Croft, son-in-law of the noble John of Havering, Seneschal of Gascony, we wish to confer on him as a special favour an ecclesiastical benefice, with or without cure of souls, in the gift of the monastery of Worcester, soon to be vacant, of value not exceeding 60 marks, and subject to no deductions. His deficiencies in Orders and in age, being in his seventeenth year or thereabouts, do not bar this, as we give him a dispensation, *ex uberiori dono gratiæ*, to accept this." (There is a marginal note here to say that the statement of age is untrue; that the boy was barely twelve in 1308, *prout per aspectum corporis apparebat.*)

The Bull is dated Bordeaux, June 6, 1306.

The letter of the Prior of Wormeley is dated April 26, 1307. A year later, on March 22, 1308, the Prior and Convent notify to the Prior of Wormeley that the living of Knightwick is vacant, and not without protest they allow it to be given to John

Boter (who is then apparently about fourteen). On March 24 the Prior of Wormeley testifies that John was duly collated and invested by him—*ipsum investientes per nostrum birettum*—and the Archdeacon of Worcester; and the public notary also testifies to the fact of the induction. A year later, however, though there had been some correspondence as to the small value of Knightwick, on March 27, 1309, John Boter himself writes. He recites the Bull; but he entirely renounces his claim. He swears on the Holy Gospels *quod pretextu harum litterarum dictos priorem et conventum nullatenus fatigabo, nec, quod in me fuerit, fatigari permittem.* And thus the affair ends.

461

THE KING ASKS THE PRIOR FOR HELP TOWARDS THE TRANSPORT OF HIS FORCES IN THE SCOTCH WAR

Folio 40, d. Nos. 461, 462. A.D. 1309

[There are several letters on this subject extending over some years, which may be of value to the student of that period. They are mostly in the Anglo-French of the time.]

" EDWARD, by the grace of God King of England, Lord of Ireland, and Duke of Aquitaine, to our beloved in God, the Prior of Worcester, greeting.

" Since we intend, with God's help, to be in Newcastle-on-Tyne very soon after next Michaelmas, and thence—*dilocques*—to go on into Scotland to win there some success over our enemies—*pur faire y locques bon exploit sur nos enemys*—which God will teach us, and since for this we must have a large supply of carriage, we pray you affectionately—*cherement*—to assist us with your carriages as much as you can, so that matters which will be of importance to us and to those who will be in our company, may not for want of carriage fail, to the damage of ourselves and of you, and of our realm, which may God avert.

" Arrange that the carriages you will send us shall come to Lincoln—*Nicole*—so that they may be there on the 5th day of October next, to be delivered to those whom we shall appoint to receive them for us—*de par nous*.

" Let us know without delay by your letters, and the bearer of this, how many carriages you are able to send us.

" Given under our privy seal at Langley, the 23rd day of August, in the third year of our reign (1309)."

462

The Reply of the Prior and Convent

After the usual address he proceeds :

" We have humbly received your letters of prayer, which to us will always be commands, containing that you intend, by God's grace, soon to enter the region of Scotland to conquer your enemies, and that you need for your supplies of food many carriages : for which reason you pray that we should assist you as much as we can, and that by the bearer of your letter we should write to you in reply what we are willing to do.

" We humbly cause your very dear lordship to know that with goodwill we will send to Lincoln two wagons with horses and harness belonging to them—*enverrons deux charrettes ove les chevaux e latyr que apent a Nicole*—on the 5th day of October next, to deliver them to those whom you shall appoint to receive them from us.

" And we pray Almighty God that He will save and protect your state to His honour and the advantage of your realm, and grant you to have victory over your enemies—*et prioms dieu omnipotent que vostre etat sauve et garde, al honeur de luy et pru du Realme, et vous dont de vos enemys victorie aver.*"

Note.—The word " pru " is written with an " e " or " o " under the "r." It is connected with *preux*, *prowess*, and appears to mean " advantage " or " glory."

486

THE KING REQUESTS A LOAN OF FOOD FROM THE CONVENT IN AID OF HIS SCOTCH WARS

Folio 43, d. No. 486. A.D. 1310

[In the margin of this letter is written by a different hand: " A royal exaction of a subsidy under the name of a loan."]

" EDWARD, by the grace of God King of England, Lord of Ireland, and Duke of Aquitaine, to our well-beloved in God, the Prior of Worcester, greeting.

" From our great desire to give our advice and assistance in the affairs of our land of Scotland, which is in great peril owing to the wickedness—*par lengressete*—of our enemies in that country, who show no sort of mercy or truth to us or to our people, we have undertaken to go into those regions in our own person, to give them advice and succour in the said affairs; and we have arranged to be, with the help of God, at Berwick-on-Tweed, on the Nativity of our Lady next approaching, with our forces in as much strength as possible; so as to go forward from that place—*pur aler avant dilloques*—to accomplish our business.

" To carry out this expedition to our honour and that of our realm, we shall require to have a large supply of food for our support and that of the army, and we pray and request you earnestly and from our heart that you will be willing to assist us with the loan of certain victuals—*eider de prest de certain vitailles.* That is to say, sixty quarters of wheat, *furment*; forty quarters of barley meal, *brees*; twenty oxen and one hundred sheep; and that these supplies should be ready for delivery to our sheriff of Worcester at the beginning of August next—*a la*

Goule * *d'aust prochain avenir*—to be conveyed to Scotland ready for our arriving there.

"And if by chance you shall not be able to provide every item—*chacune parcele*—of these victuals, will you for the love you bear us, cause to be provided otherwise what we shall need; so that we shall be provided through you with the complete amount of the victuals above named.

"Please to lay to heart, for love of us, this request and this business of ours, which is important and pressing, and to carry it out willingly and graciously; since we specially rely on you, and as you love the honour and well-being of ourselves and our realm, and the successful carrying through of this our undertaking.

"Certify us without delay by your letter, and by the bearers of this letter whom we have sent you specially for this business, how far you are willing to perform this our request, and how far we may rely on being assisted by you with a loan, in this weighty and urgent matter.

"Certify us also as to the price of the supplies you will have lent to us; and we will send back our letters patent by which we shall acknowledge that we are bound to you for their cost, to be paid at Candlemas next out of the money to be raised as the tenth, or from other sources of our realm.

"Given at Canterbury, the 25th day of June, in the third year of our reign (1310)."

* *Goule* is *gueule*, the neck or gullet; and in the sense of beginning. Is it used of any month except August?

492

THE REPLY OF THE PRIOR TO THE KING'S REQUEST FOR THE LOAN OF PROVISIONS

Folio 44, r. No. 492. A.D. 1310

"To the most noble lord, etc.

"Dearest lord, it has lately pleased your lordship to request us to make you a loan of certain provisions in aid of your war in Scotland; and we all have good will, as we ought to have, to do this in aid of you and yours as far as our knowledge and power shall extend. But we are in such great distress that we have neither knowledge nor power to feed—*chevir*—or support ourselves as we ought to do, by reason of the dearness of corn, which this year in our part of the country has taken place.

"And there has not only occurred this dearness, but other kinds of misfortunes have so hampered us that we shall not be able to recover for a long time.

"We, therefore, humbly pray your lordship that in compassion for us you will hold us excused until Michaelmas, at which time we will be ready to the utmost of our power perfectly to execute your request, which is to us a command, in the matter of provisions and all else.

"And we pray Almighty God to save and protect you, to His honour and the good of the realm, and to grant you victory over your enemies."

In 493, Gilbert de Clare, Earl of Gloucester and Hereford, demands that they should send a wagon and four horses and two men to Tewkesbury by August 15. The Prior replies that their wagons are much needed for their harvest, and *pur repariler leur eglise.* The King writes again urgently, asking for wagons to be sent to Newark by August 24. And then the Prior consents, and sends two wagons with their horses and harness—*humblement fesons a savoir que nous de bone volonte enverrons deux charrettes ove* (*avec*) *les chevaux et l'atyr qui apent.*

Other similar requests occur.

504

THE INSTALLATION OF BISHOP WALTER REYNOLDS

Folio 45, d. Nos. 502, 503, 504. A.D. 1310

[On August 11, 1310, in the second year of his consecration, the Bishop wrote to the Prior that he was anxious to complete the ceremony of his enthronization, which had been too long delayed; and on August 25 he fixed the day, Sunday, September 27. It did, however, take place on September 20. It is a little surprising that he should so earnestly request the presence of the Prior—*ad nostri honoris cumulum, vestri enim presentia ibidem gratissima nobis erit et accepta.* This correspondence is contained in 502 and 503. The account of the installation follows in 504.]

"THE venerable father Walter, by the grace of God Lord Bishop of Worcester, in the second year of his consecration, proposing to be installed in his cathedral church of Worcester on the 13th of the kalends of October, in the year of Our Lord, 1310, *D* being the dominical letter, spent the night at Kempsey.

"Brother John de Wyke, Prior of Worcester, went thither very early next morning with a goodly company of monks and esquires; and, since the Bishop wished to anticipate the crowd of people, forthwith conducted him as far as to the nearer Red Hill—*usque ad montem rubeum citeriorem.* There he left him, and hastened back to prepare himself and his Convent to meet the Bishop. The Bishop took off his shoes at the said hill, and proceeded towards the church barefoot: but went into St. Wulstan's Hospital, and presented an oblation there in the infirmary ward before the image of the saint—*apud hospitale sancti Wulstani in infirmitorio ibidem ad ipsius sancto ymaginem intravit et optulit.*

"He then went on, and entered the cemetery of

the church by the lych-gate—*per portam funerum*. Then the Prior and Convent, and also the Abbot of Pershore (no other dignitaries—*prelati*—of the diocese being present as it was still early in the morning), vested in copes, went in procession as far as the well in the cemetery to meet the Bishop, following the usual order. All then went in pairs to the door of the church. Here two strips of russet had been laid down from the steps of the porch up to the middle of the choir; and on these they walked towards the great altar. On reaching the altar the Bishop said a prayer, and made an oblation, and blessed the people. He then went to his stall near the choir, the *Te Deum Laudamus* was solemnly chanted; and . . . appointed for this occasion as commissary of . . . Lord Archdeacon of Canterbury read his commission and installed the Bishop.

"When this was done the Bishop washed his feet in the vestry, and put on his shoes, and rested for a short time in the chamber of the Lord Prior. After this, along with the abbots, priors, and other dignitaries of the diocese, he celebrated Mass at the great altar. When this was finished he went across to his breakfast in his own hall—*curia*—along with a great multitude of invited guests; and on that day he entertained the whole Convent in various rooms at his own expense. After breakfast he confirmed a great number of children.

"On the following day at about the hour of prime he offered at the great altar a most costly cope; and at each of the two shrines he made an offering.

"After this he dedicated two altars in the lower church, one in honour of the Blessed Mary, and the other in honour of St. Edmund. Next he confirmed a number of children, and celebrated High Mass;

during which, before the Gospel, he received the profession of two monks, Wulstan and Simon of Worcester, in the usual form. When Mass was ended he went into the chapter house and there preached to the Convent, and others of the clergy who wished to be present, taking as his theme 'Thou hast ravished my heart, my sister, my spouse.' "

The text is taken from the Song of Solomon iv. 9.

Note.—This document solves the archæological problem brought before the Worcester Society in January 1879 by a well-known local historian and antiquary, John Noake. " It is related," he writes, " that King Stephen raised two forts or mounts, one upon Henwick Hill, and the other on ' Red Hill, near Digley,' to command the Castle, but I cannot say," he continues, " that this ' hill near Digley ' is what we now know as Fort Royal." Now, the fact that the Bishop took off his shoes at the foot of " the nearer Red Hill," as he came in from Kempsey before going into what is now ' the Commandery,' makes it clear that Fort Royal was then called " the nearer Red Hill," and therefore that this was the " Red Hill, near Digley," on which Stephen made his fort. It adds one more certain historical reminiscence to Fort Royal Park. The name is, of course, derived from the red sandstone exposed in the original cuttings for the road, both there and higher up on the London Road. The latter was probably then known as " the further Red Hill."

As this is Bishop Walter Reynold's first appearance in the diocese, it may be well to say something about him. On the death of William of Gainsborough, the last Bishop, the Convent, as usual, requested leave from the King to elect his successor. Leave was granted ; but probably with a clear indication that no one except Walter Reynolds would be acceptable. The chapter gave the Prior the sole power to nominate : and on November 13, 1307, he named and they elected Walter Reynolds. He already held rich preferment : but was unworthy of it. He was a clerk of humble origin, not a scholar ; Professor Tout describes him as " one of the evil-living secular-minded clerks in the court of Edward I, who rose to be tutor, confidant, and favourite of the frivolous, wilful, extravagant, and dissolute young Prince." He was not approved by the Pope till February 12, 1308 ; and only then after considerable persuasion and large payments from the King. He spent little time in this diocese, and in October 1313 he became Archbishop of Canterbury. Professor Tout, in the *National Dictionary of Biography*, writes that " intellectually and morally Reynolds was, of all the mediæval Archbishops of Canterbury, the least deserving of respect."

513

IRISH ASSISTANT BISHOPS

Folio 46, d. No. 513. A.D. 1310

[There are some little episodes, not mentioned in graver histories, but which throw light on the times. An Irish Bishop, who has difficulties in his own diocese, invites himself, in December 1310, to stay with the Prior. His letter, No. 513, must be given in full.]

"Brother G., by God's permission Bishop of Annaghdown, to the reverend father in Christ, the Lord Prior of Worcester, greeting.

"In times past we have laboured in different English dioceses, exercising our episcopal functions in them; and now, having recently arrived from Ireland, and hearing of your good fame, we are coming to you that we may become acquainted with one another. We, therefore, beg that of your kindness you will admit us and a few horsemen on Thursday next to the courtesy of your hospitality."

A few years later, in August 1313, Bishop Reynolds employs him as an assistant, empowering him to consecrate churches, basilicas, altars, super-altars, and cemeteries, and to confirm children (609).

Bishop Reynolds, who spent little time in the diocese, also in February 1313 requested Roland, Archbishop of Armagh, to assist him; and he sends a mandate (570) to all clergy that they are to receive him with all honour, *prout decet tanto viro*.

There is a canny marginal memorandum on this letter in the *Liber*. It reads, "This mandate does not require us to provide him with meat and drink."

Such "procurations," as they were called, were a heavy tax. The Lateran Council of 1179 orders that reasonable procurations must be provided, and limits the number of attendants. An archbishop may not visit with more than fifty horses or men ; a bishop with more than thirty ; an archdeacon with more than seven ; or a rural dean with more than two ; and a reasonable sum of money must be accepted in lieu of procurations.

514

CORRESPONDENCE BETWEEN THE MONASTERIES OF ST. AUGUSTINE'S, CANTERBURY AND WORCESTER ABOUT JOHN DE ST. GERMAN

Folio 46, r. Nos. 514, 515. A.D. 1310

"To the men of holy religion and our very dear brothers in Christ, the Lord Prior and Convent of the cathedral church of Worcester, their devoted servants in Christ, Ralph, by Divine permission Abbot of the monastery of St. Augustine at Canterbury, and the convent of the same place, salvation in Him Who was born from the Virgin's womb.

"Although by the obligation of our brotherly union we are bound to study everything which affects the honour of our holy congregation, yet we are specially affected by your kindnesses; in that it is from your benevolence and with your consent, that our venerable brother John de St. German, a brother of yours, whom we embrace with the fullest affection, has of his grace diligently laboured among us for our instruction.

"He is one of whom, for nobility of conversation and character, and for every mark of virtue, in all our neighbourhood widespread fame has so sounded the praise, that his absence will be deservedly deplored by all who know him.

"Now, therefore, that, much against our will, he is leaving us, and devoting himself to scholastic studies, since he intends by his labours to advance the credit of the Order, we most affectionately appeal to your reverence on his behalf, that inasmuch as his own means, as we have learned, are insufficient, you will regard this distinguished man with the eyes of your liberality, and extend a helping hand to relieve his needs; so that by your gracious assistance he may with honour complete what he has planned to do for the praise of God and the credit of his Order.

"Our own monastery, for certain well-known reasons, is weighed down with debt: and we are further burdened with the expenses of two of our brethren, whom out of reverence for John de St. German we have sent with him to "the schools" (*scolas*, the University of Paris). We are, therefore, to our regret, unable to provide for him ourselves; though in very truth we have the strongest desire to do everything for his advantage and honour to the utmost of our power.

"May your holy congregation long prosper in happiness and constantly grow in Divine grace.

"Given in our chapter house, December 10, 1310."

515

The Reply

"To the men of honoured religion, and our most dear friends in Christ, the Lord Ralph, by the grace of God the Abbot of the monastery of St. Augustine, Canterbury, and the Convent of the same place, brother John, Prior of the cathedral church of Worcester, greeting and the attainment of all prosperity with the Saviour's grace.

"For the goodwill of your holy congregation which has extended so largely over us the branches of its affection, and has with such deep and welcome consideration regarded our honour, and also for the courtesies and kindnesses so liberally conferred by you in the past on our beloved brother John de St.

German, kindnesses to be continued as we hope in the future, and further for the burden of expense which, as out of reverence for him, as we gather from your letter, you are bearing in sending to the university your two brothers, for all these things we offer you our heartiest possible thanks.

"But with the utmost confidence we assure you that ever since our brother aforesaid has been in Paris we believe that as regards all that is necessary he is and has been sufficiently supplied; that whenever hitherto he has needed anything else his want has been supplied, and that when it becomes known to us by his own letters that he is in want, we will endeavour to the utmost of our power to assist him. It is our wish to disregard any excuse which our poverty suggests as to the expense, and with God's help, as place and time may serve, to promote his interest, and those of our church.

"May your holy congregation always be strong in Christ, for His continued, happy and wholesome worship.

"Given at Worcester, January 14, A.D. 1311."

520

A CITATION ISSUED BY THE COLLECTORS OF FIRST-FRUITS TO THEIR COMMISSARIES TO COME AND RENDER THEIR ACCOUNTS

Folio 47, d. No. 520. A.D. 1311

[The following letter illustrates the heavy tax levied on benefices to supply money for the Pope, and how it was enforced.]

"The Collectors of the fruits of the first year of ecclesiastical benefices vacant in England, appointed by the Apostolic See, to the man of discretion, the official of the Bishop of Worcester, or his locum tenens, salvation in the Author of salvation.

"Although we have sufficiently notified all those rectors, vicars, and others holding benefices in farm—*firmarios*—whose names are contained in the first schedule annexed hereto, that they must satisfy us as to the fruits of the benefices which they hold for themselves or in farm, fruits owing to our lord the Pope by reason of the vacancy, and due at a stated place and time now past, under stated canonical penalties and censures imposed by us, yet nevertheless these same rectors, vicars, and others holding benefices in farm, have up to the present time not cared to satisfy us as to those fruits. For this reason we have, as justice demands, excommunicated them by these writings.

"For these reasons we commit to you, with our strict injunctions and commands, with reference to the aforesaid rectors, vicars, and those holding benefices in farm, all and each, exempt and non-exempt, the duty of publicly and solemnly, in their own churches and in other churches and places as shall seem expedient to you, denouncing and causing them to be denounced, on all Sundays and festivals, until they shall have satisfied us respecting the said fruits, or shall have deserved to obtain from us in legal form the benefit of absolution.

" Those, however, who have not been otherwise admonished, whose names you will find at the end of the aforesaid schedule, both exempt and non-exempt, you are to warn canonically and effectually to satisfy us concerning the fruits of the benefices which they hold for themselves or in farm, fruits now owing to our lord the Pope on account of the vacancies of those benefices, before the octave of Easter in London at our hostel, or on the day following the said octave they must show reasonable cause, if they have any, why they are not bound to make this payment.

" Otherwise these men, whom from this time, as from that, in these writings we excommunicate, you are to denounce and cause to be denounced publicly as excommunicate, until you are informed by our letters of their absolution ; and you are to sequestrate, and keep and cause to be kept in strict sequestration, all fruits, rents and income of their benefices until they shall have adequately satisfied us as to the said fruits.

" You are also to cite the Prior of Worcester, and Master Thomas de Westone, our commissaries, that on the aforesaid day they shall appear with full information before us, at the place named before, to render us full accounts, and satisfy us as to all that they have received, administered and done on our commission, and, moreover, to be ready to do further and to receive what may be required, within reason, by our office for them to do either in person or through others.

"As to the day on which you receive this letter, and as to what you shall have done as to its contents, and the names of those whom you have denounced or admonished, to be given in a schedule appended to your report, you are to take care that we shall be clearly and fully informed by your letters patent giving all these details, before or at latest on the aforesaid day.

"Given at London, the 12th of the month of March 1311."

528

AN OLD QUARREL AMICABLY SETTLED BETWEEN OUR MONASTERY AND THAT OF ST. AUGUSTINE'S, BRISTOL

Folio 49, r, *et seq.* Nos. 528–534. A.D. 1311

THIS correspondence can only be given in a highly abridged form. I have sent it *in extenso* to the Bristol and Gloucester Archæological Society.

In 528 the Abbot of St. Augustine's, Bristol, begs the Chapter of Worcester to sanction the appropriation of the church of Wotton to relieve their poverty. He adds that they have furnished their proctors in London with full powers, and hopes that the Worcester Chapter will do the same, to refer matters in dispute to the Bishop, so that *si vos in aliquibus gravavimus . . . amodo inter nos cedantur omnes altercationes.*

In 529 the Prior writes that they have instructed their proctors to confer with those from Bristol and with the Bishop, and report on their return.

531 is the Bishop's letter to his official, Benedict de Pastone, reporting the facts stated by the Abbot and Convent of St. Augustine's, Bristol, that their church is *pro majori parte funditus diruta, in parte residua gravem minatur ruinam*: that from their position in a great port, and a famous city, great demands are made on their hospitality; that from the persecution of certain powerful persons they have been robbed of nearly a third of their substance; and that they are grievously pressed with debts. They, therefore, beg that to enable them to carry on the good work of the monastery the Bishop will appropriate to them the church of Wotton.

The Bishop goes on to state that his careful inquiries

show that these statements are true: so much so that sometimes the monks had nothing for dinner—*hora prandii nihil esum vel potum paratum habentes*—; they were compelled to send into the city of Bristol to beg or borrow food. He himself is well disposed to help them, but will not act without the canonical sanction of the chapter.

In 534 the Abbot and Convent of St. Augustine's write to our Prior, saying that since questions have lately arisen between their two houses both as to the right of visitation, *sede vacante*, and as to a certain cope, with the result that their mutual affection was cooling, they propose to admit the Prior to exercise the office of visitation as far as the laws permit, and Boniface's composition prescribes: and they will submit to the Bishop's decision in the matter of the cope.

Peace is to reign, *omni lite et judiciali strepitu interim dormiente.*—Chapter House, Bristol, September 27, 1311.

545

LEVY OF FOUR PENCE IN THE MARK BY THE PROVINCIAL COUNCIL ON ALL ECCLESIASTICAL INCOMES, TO FORM A CENTRAL FUND TO MEET EMERGENCIES

Folio 52, r. No. 545. A.D. 1312

[This is interesting as the establishment of a Central Church Fund by the Provincial Council taxing themselves at 2½ per cent. on their incomes.]

" WALTER, by Divine permission Bishop of Worcester, to his beloved son, the Custos of Sequestrations in our Archdeaconry of Worcester, salvation, grace, and blessing.

" We have received a mandate from the venerable father, Robert, by the grace of God the Lord Archbishop of Canterbury, Primate of all England, with content as follows:

" Robert, by Divine permission Archbishop of Canterbury, Primate of all England, to our venerable brother, Walter, by the grace of God Lord Bishop of Worcester, greeting and brotherly charity in the Lord.

" In our provincial Council, being held at this present time in London with a view to forming a certain reserve fund—*aliquale depositum*—from which prompt assistance could be given to meet urgent needs of our own or of the churches of our province, we have decided that four pence out of every mark of property held in community and of the ecclesiastical benefices in our province, rated according to the last assessment, should be collected: this was agreed to by the clergy of our province, and was settled by the advice and assent of our venerable brethren present at the Council, those of the vicars and proctors acting for yourself and others of our brothers and suffragans who were absent. It was decided that the levy so imposed should be collected by you and each of our suffragans in their own cities and dioceses, at the time stated below; such reserve fund to be called upon when there was urgent necessity or obvious advantage.

"We therefore lay on your fraternity by our injunction and command, the duty of canonically compelling all ecclesiastical persons subject to your jurisdiction and living therein, to pay these pence above-named, and the arrears of the procurations of the Lord Abbot of Lagny and Richard de Vaure, and of the pence imposed at an earlier date to meet the necessities of the churches of our province. Half of the aforesaid fourpence is to be paid before the feast of St. Margaret the Virgin (July 13), and the remaining half before the feast of St. Mathias the Apostle (February 24) next occurring; and also the arrears aforesaid as stated in the mandates of the Lords Abbot and Richard, and ourselves, and that without any diminution whatever; and the said four pence are to be kept in a safe place, until you shall have received from us other instructions. The arrears, however, named above, you are without any delay to transmit to the Prior of Holy Trinity, London, whom we have otherwise deputed to receive them.

"You are faithfully to inform us by your letters patent giving all detail, what you shall have done in the foregoing matters before the dates above-named.

"Given in the aforesaid Council in London, XI Kalendis Junii, Anno Domini 1312, the eighteenth year of our consecration.

"This mandate we commit to you, to be faithfully

carried out in its tenor and form in all its articles, ordering you to certify us suitably by your letters patent, giving all details what you shall have done, that we may be able to certify our venerable father aforesaid at the proper time.

"Given at Bredon, Kal. Junii, in the year of Our Lord as above, in the fourth year of our consecration.

"Bredon, June 1, 1312."

Such was the Archbishop's letter, and the resolution of the Council of the Province, dated May 22, 1312. But the King had heard of the intention and wrote to the Abbot, Priors and others in charge of monasteries in the King's patronage, forbidding them to pay this tax as an infringement of his rights. This inhibition is printed in Wilkins's *Concilia*, II, 420, as *Ex Reg. magno Wigorn.* I do not know whether it exists elsewhere than in our *Liber Albus*. It is headed "The inhibition of our lord the King: that no collection shall be made in the aforesaid Council without his being consulted."

546

THE ARCHBISHOP ON THE TROUBLES OF THE REALM

Folio 52, d. No. 546. A.D. 1312

[In 1312, and the years immediately preceding, England was in sore distress from bands of robbers and intestine quarrels. The Archbishop, Robert Winchelsey, anxious for peace and tranquillity, wrote a letter, No. 546, to our Bishop, of which the following is an abstract.]

"We know," he writes, "that the Author of peace cannot, except in times of peace, be fitly worshipped. This famous realm of England, which used to rejoice in the beauty of peace, is now afflicted and rent and divided. We intend therefore, with the advice and consent of our suffragans, to invoke the aid of heaven against the disturbers of peace, and to grant heavenly rewards to those who foster and defend it.

"We, therefore, charge you to excommunicate, solemnly and publicly, all such disturbers of peace, and especially those who plunder clerks, and all who share their crime. This is to be done in all the churches of your city and diocese: the bells are to be tolled; the cross lifted up; the candles lighted and extinguished; and none can absolve them, except *in mortis articulo*, save the Bishop alone.

"For the truly penitent, who foster and defend the peace of the realm, and thrice repeat for it the Lord's Prayer, and the invocation of the Blessed Virgin, we, and our suffragans present in this our provincial Council, each grant twenty days of indulgence, two hundred days in all.

"Moreover, since a just and merciful God allows the fire of His wrath to blaze against the sins of men, and for the sins of some sends vengeance on all, we fear future perils for our realm, unless God in His mercy looks on us, and applies a healing remedy.

"Therefore, since the God of pity even in His just wrath remembers mercy, and attends to the prayers of the faithful, we order that solemn processions shall be held for prayer.

"All the members of our cathedral and collegiate churches are to meet before Mass alternately on Wednesdays and Fridays, and go in procession to the church, and subsequently in the Mass, they are to pour out their prayers to the Lord, whose anger for our sins we justly dread, that He would take the helm of this kingdom—*regni hujus gubernacula diriget*—and for His mercy's sake grant us secure and lasting peace.

"Other clergy in their parishes, at least once a week, shall form similar processions for prayers, at hours when the largest number of their people can assemble.

"We, therefore, order that in your city and diocese, such processions and Masses shall be observed, under ecclesiastical penalties if required, until further notice.

"London, May 22, 1312."

[What a glimpse this gives us into the discipline and teaching by which the Church, in spite of all its shortcomings and crimes, did, through long centuries, keep God and His eternal laws and judgments before the minds of our rough and lawless race. Who can estimate the debt our nation owes to the Church of the Middle Ages ?]

547

THE KING'S INHIBITION

Folio 53, r. No. 547. A.D. 1312

"EDWARD, etc., to his beloved in Christ, the Abbots, Priors, and others of the houses of religion in the province of Canterbury which are in our patronage, and to their proctors, about to meet immediately in London, greeting.

"We have understood from certain persons that the venerable father Robert, Archbishop of Canterbury, is striving with all his power, and intending to induce you, along with the rest of his clergy of the aforesaid province, to consent to a certain levy or collection to be imposed by his own authority on you and the clergy.

"Since, therefore, an assessment or grant of such a levy or collection, if made, without our consent being asked, on the property of your houses, which were founded by the alms of our progenitors, formerly kings of England, manifestly tends to the diminution of the aforesaid alms, and to the prejudice of our Crown, we command you by your fidelity to us, and we strictly forbid you to assent to any levy or collection made, as stated above, from you or others of the aforesaid clergy; or that you should give your consent and assent, to making any contribution to a collection of this sort along with others of the clergy, if it should happen that they consent on their behalf, without our having been consulted.

"*Teste me ipso*, at Newcastle-on-Tyne, May 1, 1312."

552

A DISPENSATION FROM THE PRIOR TO A WORCESTER MONK AT OXFORD TO OBSERVE THE UNIVERSITY STATUTES AND TAKE ANY LAWFUL OATH ON INCEPTION, IN A LETTER TO THE CHANCELLOR

Folio 53, d. No. 552. A.D. 1312

"To the man of excellent discretion, the Lord Chancellor of the University of Oxford, brother John, the humble Prior of the cathedral church of Worcester, wishes the joy of safety here and hereafter—*salutis gaudium utriusque*—in Him from whom all wisdom for ever flows.

"Since we well understand that, on grounds both of law and of reason, no one can be excused from the burdens attached to a position from which he desires to obtain advantage and honour, we grant special permission to our beloved fellow-monk and brother, Ranulph de Catthrop, to observe the statutes and customs of the University aforesaid, so far as they affect a religious who is a scholar; and for that purpose we permit him to take any lawful oath on his approaching inception, saving the regular institutes of our Order. To you and to all who have honoured us and our Order by promoting the said inception we give our heartiest possible thanks."

554

A DISPUTE ABOUT THE POSSESSION OF ST. WULSTAN'S PASTORAL STAFF

Folio 53, d. Nos. 554, 555. A.D. 1312

[The hospital of St. Wulstan was an ancient foundation just outside the city walls. It is now known as the Commandery.]

THE Bishop of Worcester writes to the Prior with the usual greetings:

"We have received a complaint from the Warden and Brethren of our hospital of St. Wulstan, stating that, although from ancient times they had obtained a certain pastoral staff, which formerly, we are informed, belonged to St. Wulstan the Confessor, our patron, for requesting alms and receiving them for the support of the hospital aforesaid, yet you unjustly prevent them from obtaining the said staff and receiving alms as they had been accustomed to do: indeed, that you have taken the staff itself from them, to the great injury of the hospital, and the notorious diminution of its hospitality; and, if the facts are so, to the manifest peril of your souls.

"We, therefore, affectionately advise and exhort you in the Lord that if the above statements are founded on truth, you should freely allow them to have the staff aforesaid for such alms as they have hitherto used it for, at any rate until our coming, which we hope will shortly take place if God permits.

"Reply to us in writing what you decide to do in this matter.

"Given in London, V Kalends of October.

"London, September 27, 1312."

555

The Reply

After the usual formal address the Prior writes:

"We have lately received through your official a letter from your reverend paternity, containing an insinuation—*suggestionem*—from the Warden and Brethren of the hospital of St. Wulstan that we have taken away from them a certain staff of St. Wulstan, unjustly as they assert; and your request that if these statements are founded on truth, we should, at least until you come hither, of our charity allow them to have the staff aforesaid, and to use it for the alms that it brings in; and that we should reply by our letter what we are going to do in this matter.

"We therefore humbly signify to your lordship that the insinuation of the Warden and Brethren of the hospital aforesaid has no foundation of truth. In fact, the staff they speak of has never up to this moment been for a day or night or an hour out of our custody, and in the possession of any one else; it is, therefore, clear that what never was theirs could not have been taken from them.

"But although at their request permission has been occasionally granted them to collect for their own advantage offerings made at the same staff, they now claim this favour, to the prejudice of our church and yours, as if it were a right of their own; and we dare not, on grounds of conscience, grant them this kindness in future. Indeed, by such action your Mother Church, which has hitherto been incontestably free, would be placed in miserable slavery to her daughter, which we hope is far from your wish.

"Moreover, when in defence of the rights of your church and ours we brought a just action at law against the Warden and Brethren about the exhumation of a certain Franciscan friar, since they do not possess the right of sepulture, they brought forward in the said action about the exhumation, in order to restrict the rights of sepulture possessed by your church, a counter-charge of aggression on their rights —*exceptionem spoliationis*—thus adding injury to injury.

"Wherefore we humbly implore you as our father and immediate lord, that you will make these Warden and Brethren—who though yours are not yours as we are—to desist from such injustice and provocation, so that we may enjoy the peace we long for, and under your wings may more freely serve the Lord.

"Let not your holiness marvel that we gently—*modeste*—resist their presumption, for they do not shrink from using any far-fetched pretext for invading our rights.

"Farewell, etc.

"Written and sealed with the common seal in the Chapter House of Worcester on the feast of St. Luke the Evangelist, A.D. 1312, and the letter was closed."

AN INQUIRY INTO THE FINANCE OF THE MONASTERY OF WORCESTER

Folio 54, d. No. 562. A.D. 1313

This is a detailed and important inquiry. Only an abridged report can be given here. In 561 the official of the Bishop informs the rural deans of Worcester and Droitwich that the Bishop has received a statement from the Convent into the truth of which he directs inquiry to be made. The Bishop's letter is dated "London, December 21, 1312." He, therefore, directs the Deans to summon fit persons to appear before him in the cathedral and give evidence.

In 562 the official's report is given at great length. It recites the letter from the Convent to the Bishop, pleading that "their monastery, founded in the famous city of Worcester in times past by the munificent kindness of kings and the devotion of many of the faithful, was sufficiently wealthy to meet the claims of hospitality and the needs of fifty monks who were serving God therein: but that as a result of hostility and plunder they had lost, without fault of theirs, eight manors and five noble churches; that at the present time, through innumerable devices of their enemies under far-fetched excuses they were being deprived of their possessions and goods; that from the conflux of people to Worcester partly for legal business, partly because of the bridge which provided the only and inevitable road for forty-eight leagues for those who crossed the Severn, the demands on their hospitality had increased; and that the Convent is further burdened with heavy debt; so that a reduction of their hospitality or of their services of God, to the scandal of the whole Church, and the eternal disgrace of the monks, unless some speedy remedy be found, was inevitable."

On these grounds the Convent have requested the Bishop to appropriate to them the church of Dodderhill. The Bishop, therefore, orders the official, as stated above, to inquire into the facts.

Then follows the official's report. He had summoned a large number of clergy and laymen, whose names are given, from the deaneries of Worcester and Droitwich, in the latter of which Dodderhill is situated. They are all sworn ; and they find in succession that the first article is true, viz. that the monastery formerly amply endowed, has now lost thirteen manors, viz. Pendock, Mutton, Lench, Clemculum in Ireland, Lockesley, Burton, Laugherne, Pelbeworth, Grimenhull, Bradecote, Spechesleye, and Hesbury Ambo. They have also lost six churches : Wolverhampton and Westbury (which have been recently made collegiate), Dodderhill, Wolverley, Overbury, and Bliche, which are parish churches. These manors and churches provided a third part of the revenues of the monastery.

The second article they also confirm in much detail. That their possessions and goods *per varia indictamenta falsa et multiplices extorsiones iniquas consumuntur et minuuntur injuste est ita notorium et publicum et manifestum in dyoscesi Wigorniensi quod nulla potest tergiversatione celari.*

The third article as to the conflux of people is similarly confirmed from their own knowledge. The monthly meeting of the *comitatus*, the Justices, the Chapters, the *dies amoris* (i.e. meeting for amicable adjustments), causes referred by the Roman court to be inquired into, are matters of daily occurrence. There is no bridge over the Severn between Gloucester and Bridgenorth, which are forty-eight leagues apart, except at Worcester, which is halfway between them.

The fourth article as to debt is also true of their own knowledge. The Prior and Convent are diligent and sagacious in business: but the pressure is unavoidable, and help must be given to avoid the catastrophe indicated above.

This is dated January 12, 1313.

582

CITATION OF THE PRIOR AND CONVENT FOR THE CONSOLIDATION OF THE CHURCH OF HAMPTON MEYSEY

Folio 58, d. No. 582. A.D. 1313

[The consolidation here spoken of was the fusion of the income of the vicar with that of the rector. It was successfully resisted by the Convent in the interest of the parish.]

"THE official of the venerable father Walter by the grace of God Lord Bishop of Worcester, the special commissary of the said father in the matter hereinafter described, to the man of discretion the dean of Worcester, salvation in the Author of Salvation.

"Since an inquiry respecting the articles contained —*comprehensis*—in a petition of John, the Rector of the church of Hampton Meysey, which he lately presented to the said father for the consolidation of the vicarage which for a long time has existed in that church, has been made on the mandate of the said father, and appears prima facie (in the text *facere*) and fully to be in favour of the said Rector, and for his obtaining the object of his petition, we enjoin and command you to notify and peremptorily cite the Prior and Chapter of the cathedral church of Worcester to appear before us in that cathedral church on the 7th legal day—*die juridico*—after the Sunday on which the office *Lætare Jerusalem* is sung, to produce reasonable cause if they have any, against such restoration—*redintegratio*—or consolidation of this nature, to propose it in legal form, and to establish it as far as right permits; also to produce in the interests of justice (*judicialiter*, perhaps 'in court') any register that they may possess of the separation—*sectio*—of the said church, or of a regularly appointed payment

—*assignatio*—for the aforesaid vicarage ; and also to prosecute and finish any cause or causes of this sort effectually, with power to continue and extend them till the final settlement of the business on account of the danger involved in delay in such affairs, and finally to accept the decision which justice will recommend.

"What you shall have done in this business you are to certify to us at the time and place above-stated by your letters patent in full detail.

"Given at Blockley, on the 7th of the Kalends of April, A.D. 1313."

599

A PENSION GRANTED TO MASTER JOHN DE STRATFORD, CLERK

Folio 60, d. No. 599. A.D. 1313

[There was a very distinguished monk of Worcester, John de Stratford. A few years later a distinguished John de Stratford, a Doctor of Civil Law, was clerk to the King, and became Archdeacon of Lincoln, Bishop of Winchester, Chancellor and Archbishop of Canterbury (see 661). This document provides a strong argument against the identity.]

"To all Christ's faithful to whose knowledge the present letter shall have come, brother John, Prior of the cathedral church of Worcester, and the Convent of the same place, eternal salvation in the Lord.

"In return for the labour, protection, and wholesome counsel which our beloved and kind master John de Stratford will give in future for the advantage of the said church and ourselves, we hereby unanimously grant that whensoever he wishes to stay with us he shall be honourably entertained at our expense.

"And we further grant that every year five marks in equal portions at the feasts of St. Michael and the Annunciation, shall be paid at the hands of our cellarer for the time being, to the same John or his certified attorney, who shall bring a receipt for the same in the priory of Worcester, until he shall have been provided with a sufficient ecclesiastical benefice.

"In testimony whereof our common seal is hereto appended.

"Given at Worcester, on the vigil of St. Matthew the Apostle and Evangelist, A.D. 1313."

600

JOHN DE STRATFORD'S OATH THAT HE WILL FAITHFULLY DISCHARGE HIS DUTY

Folio 60, d. No. 600. A.D. 1313

"LET all men know that I, John de Stratford, clerk, bind myself by these presents to my masters the Prior and Convent of Worcester, that in all causes and concerns of their own and of their church I will give faithful counsel, protection, and assistance, and also faithful and diligent obedience (at their expense, however), as often and wherever I shall have been lawfully requested so to do by any person or persons authorized by them to make the request.

"I have also sworn on God's holy gospels that without their consent I will never reveal to any living person, by word or deed, directly or indirectly, their own secrets or those of their church, however known to me, or anything which may possibly be to the prejudice of themselves or their church.

"Moreover, I have sworn that if I know that any person or persons are plotting evil against these my masters aforesaid or their church, or that in other way evil is imminent, I will defeat and annul it to the utmost of my power, or I will put these my masters on their guard, or cause them to be on their guard, against these plots.

"In testimony whereof my seal is appended.

"Given at Worcester, on the feast of St. Mathias the Apostle, A.D. 1313."

Note.—This, as will be seen from 628, is almost identical with the usual form of oath taken by all pensioners of the Convent.

605

THE PRIOR CONGRATULATES THE BISHOP, WALTER REYNOLDS, ON BEING PROMOTED TO THE ARCH-BISHOPRIC OF CANTERBURY

Folio 61, r. No. 605. A.D. 1313

"To the most reverend, etc., obedience and reverence with the honour due to so great a father.

"To your fatherly lordship, under whose rule we have always rejoiced in plenty and in peace, we offer our humble and devout thanks. We are well assured that though your translation to the high post of the church of Canterbury is to us, who have tasted somewhat of the immensity of your sweetness and benevolence, both a loss and a source of sorrow, yet the assurance of further grace, which granted us a man so great, that not to us only, but to the father of the whole Church it seemed good to call you to the rule and defence of the church of Canterbury, has relieved and consoled us. We are like a woman in the pains of childbirth, who when she has brought forth her child, remembers no more the anguish because a man is born into the world. From our hearts we rejoice with you; and we hope that we, who have already been protected by you from our enemies, may, now that you have reached the eminence of an archbishop, be defended with even greater affection.

"Above all we sincerely entreat your Holiness that, if it please you, before you retire from the court you will finally deal with our petitions, for the advantage of our church, laid before you by the bearer of these presents, and all other matters which he may request from you and which may seem to your Holiness to be expedient.

"May the Most High direct and guide you to eternal glory."

619

CONDITIONS FOR GRANTING ABSOLUTION TO ONE WHO HAD ASSAULTED A PRIEST

Folio 62, d. No. 619. A.D. 1313

"To the reverend father in Christ, Walter, by the grace of God Lord Archbishop of Canterbury, Primate of all England, his humble and devoted son, brother John de Wyke, Prior of the cathedral church of Worcester, the ready spirit of obedience with all reverence and honour.

"Simon le Buttare, of Ombersley, the bearer of these presents, of the diocese of Worcester, has informed us that you have deigned to confer on him the benefit of absolution for the act of laying violent hands on William Lawe, Chaplain, committed by him; on condition, however, that it was made known to you by our letters that peace and concord between them had been begun and re-established.

"We, therefore, signify to your lordship, by these presents, that peace and concord between the said Simon and William, with reference to this act of violence, have been re-established as appears, to the fullest extent, from the confession of the said William made before us.

"In testimony whereof we transmit these letters, closed and open, sealed with our seal, to your reverend lordship.

"Given at Worcester, on the 9th of the Kalends of April, in the year of Our Lord, 1313."

624

AN OUTRAGE AND AN EXCOMMUNICATION

Folio 63, r. No. 624. A.D. 1313

"WALTER (of Maidstone), by Divine permission Bishop of Worcester, to his beloved sons in Christ, the Sacrist of our church of Worcester, and the Dean of Christianity of the same place, salvation, grace, and blessing.

"The horror of dire savagery, which on our first entrance on our diocese has sounded in our ears, has stirred the depths of our heart, and has given us a foretaste of the cup of bitterness, which rightly challenges us to claim that there shall be canonical punishment.

"For we have received information, clamorously brought to us by trustworthy men, that when a certain Thomas of Powick, quite recently escaping from the prison of our lord the King in the castle of Worcester, in fear of imminent death, had taken refuge in our church of Worcester, hoping there, like a suckling at its mother's breast, to have the certainty of a protection that could not fail, some sons of iniquity, ceasing not their toil in destroying their own salvation, not sparing their own mother's heart, rushed in upon the said Thomas, well known, as is stated, to be there established as a fugitive within the precincts of the said monastery for the sake of the refuge and immunity it offered, from its limits dragged him out, with violence, as is asserted; and, we relate it with sorrow, they have handed him over to the prison of the secular power; and contrary to the immunity of ecclesiastical liberty they have detained and still detain him in chains and with stripes.

"We, therefore, appointed, however unworthy we may be, to repel and avenge encroachments on the rights of that church, and being neither able nor willing to connive at and pass over the audacity of a crime so great, since it has been wickedly perpetrated not only to the serious prejudice of the liberty of the church, but also to the reproach of ourselves and our clergy, lay on you, jointly and severally in virtue of the said obedience, and under pain of canonical punishment, our firm injunction and command, that the aforesaid malefactors, who beyond all question have fallen, to their condemnation, under the sentence of greater excommunication promulgated by the holy fathers against those who trespass on ecclesiastical liberties, have been and are thus by the fact of the said crime excommunicate.

"And in the aforesaid our church of Worcester and other churches of that city, and in its neighbourhood, on Sundays and feast days, in your processions, preachings, and solemn services, in presence of clergy and the people, at times when the greatest numbers are present, bells being struck, candles lit and extinguished, cross being carried, and every solemnity in your power in such a matter being employed, you are to denounce them collectively and cause them to be denounced by others; and you are to admonish them, that within the space of six days reckoned continuously from the time of the aforesaid admonition, they are freely to restore to the same church, safe and sound, the said Thomas who had been, as above-stated, violently dragged out; and they are to make suitable satisfaction to the unity of the Holy Mother Church which they have so wickedly injured; and abstain in future from all similar acts and cunning designs.

628

THE OATH TAKEN BY EVERY ONE WHO IS GRANTED A PENSION

Folio 63, d. No. 628.

" Master A. de B., you will swear on these holy gospels of God, that from this day forward, to the limit of your powers and according to your knowledge, in all causes and businesses of ours and of our church, that are brought before an ecclesiastical court, in the provinces of Canterbury and York, you will give your aid and counsel and obedience, diligently and faithfully, to be remunerated at our expense. Also that when you shall have been duly requested to come hither on our business or that of our church you will make no frivolous excuse or knowingly shelter yourself by such means. Also that you will never, without our consent having been given, reveal for evil designs against us, to any living creature, the secrets of ourselves or our church, however they have become known to you, or any matter or matters which may in any degree prejudice us or our church.

" Also that if you shall have heard or have reason to conclude that any person or persons are designing evil against us and our church, or that any evil is impending for us or our church, you will to the best of your power bring it to naught, or, according to our agreement, you will warn or cause to be warned thereof us or our successors.

" Also that if it shall happen that you are promoted to any pensionary benefice of ours you will resign the present pension.

" So may God help you and these holy Gospels of God."

643

THE APPROPRIATION OF POWICK TO GREAT MALVERN, AND OF THORNBURY TO TEWKESBURY

Folios 65, 15. Nos. 643–645, 154. A.D. 1315

[The *Liber Albus* contains details of many appropriations of the endowments of parish churches to the support of monasteries, and the setting aside a portion of the income for a vicar. I will give here the details of two such appropriations.]

Bishop Walter Maidstone grants the appropriation in the following deed, which is submitted to the Prior and Convent for confirmation:

"The monastery of Great Malvern was originally endowed with the possessions they now hold, and also with certain manors and churches, which are enumerated in the deed. All of these, without fraud, deceit or fault of the monks, have been finally taken from them and lost in the commotions of wars and devastation of property in Wales and in England. The monastery is no longer able to support twenty-six monks and thirty resident poor, and meet the claims of hospitality. Moreover, the constant demands from the popes—*prevalens impositio summorum pontificum*—and the extortion by secular princes, have involved them in a burden of debt. Unless a speedy remedy is applied it will be necessary to diminish the number of the monks and of the poor, and thus curtail the service of God. The Convent on these grounds request that the Bishop will appropriate to their use the church of Powick and all its revenues on the cession or decease of the Rector.

"We, therefore, opening our fatherly heart—

paterna viscera reserantes—to this petition, after full inquiry, legal proof, and discussion with our chapter on the truth of these statements, with the assent and unanimous wish of the chapter, make this grant by the grace of the Holy Spirit, to the honour of the holy and undivided Trinity, the praise of the glorious Virgin, and the honour of all the Saints.

"The grant is made for the continuance of Divine worship by twenty-six monks, for the maintenance of thirty poor, and to bear the burden of hospitality, which, on account of the distance of other inaccessible places, affects and injures their monastery more than others, and towards the debts arising from impositions, extortions, and other pressures. We, therefore, grant the church of Powick, with all its rights and revenues, on the cession or decease of the Rector, to the Prior and Convent of Great Malvern, confirming this appropriation with pontifical authority, reserving all rights for ourselves, our successors, and other dignities and rights of visitation, and four marks of payment; also one mark to the church of Worcester offered freely by the Convent of Malvern, as a sign of subjection, and to recompense them for temporal loss. A portion for the vicariate, which we estimate at twelve marks, is to be secured; and the right of presentation to us of a suitable person preserved to the Convent of Great Malvern."

This deed was signed by the Bishop in London on November 14, 1314; and approved by the chapter on January 15, 1315.

It illustrates the endowment of a vicarage insisted on by the Bishop, when the monastery becomes the Rector.

The subject, however, of the endowment of a vicarage is so interesting that I will give an abstract of an inquiry and settlement of the exact sources of the income reserved for the vicar in another case, that of Thornbury, a living appropriated in the same year, 1315, to the abbey of Tewkesbury. This is from document 129.

In this instance 25 marks was reserved for the Vicar. The report is as follows:

"By a subsequent inquiry, made through clergy of the deanery and laymen of the parish, who had full knowledge of all the income, lesser tithes, portions, rights and belongings of the church, whether the offerings, income or other sources, minute tithes for altar service, viz. tithes of milk, wool, lambs, calves, bullocks, cheeses, pigs, fowls, doves, geese, cider, flax, hemp, garden stuff, with the tithes of hay (except from the demesne meadows of the lady Simonde) we found that the value of the tithes above enumerated amounted to 18 marks and 10 shillings.

"We are desirous that the rest of the income of the vicarage be fully supplied. The wax offered in devotion and reverence, for the Blessed Virgin Mary, mother of God, whose image is situated in the chancel of that church, and money in coin or in mass of silver or gold, or coming in any form; and a sufficient manse, lately occupied by a man of the name of Zelibroun, and a garden close to the manse, formerly belonging to the Rector, are assigned to produce the rest of the income."

They are of opinion that these sources of income produce 25 marks, and are sufficient for the Vicar to meet all liabilities. The Vicar is admonished to be content with this, and to make no further demand on the monastery. He must pay the Archdeacon's procurations, cathedral and synodal dues, cost of lights, procuring and repairing books, vestments, and other necessary ornaments of the church formerly provided by the Rector, and to bear all ordinary burdens. For repair and construction of the chancel, and extraordinary burdens, the Vicar is to be rated at 15 marks. The 4 marks paid to the Bishop, *sede plena*, or to the Prior, *sede vacante*, are also excepted.

This is dated Tewkesbury, August 11, 1315.

[One cannot help reflecting how difficult it must have been for a vicar to collect his income, consisting of so many different things, from so many different individuals, and at such irregular times.]

659

A TESTIMONIAL FROM THE UNIVERSITY OF PARIS TO A WORCESTER STUDENT

Folio 67, d. No. 659. A.D. 1315

[The University of Paris was at this time the most famous centre of learning. Post-graduates thronged thither to acquire the latest learning. Among these was John de St. German, who had been elected by the chapter as bishop to succeed Godfrey Giffard, in 1302, but was refused by the Pope. He had been Lecturer in St. Augustine's Monastery at Canterbury in 1308 (397–399), and had thence gone to Paris (514, 515) in 1311, and now (1315) returns to England.]

"To the venerable father in Christ, by the grace of God Lord Prior of the cathedral of Worcester and the Convent of the same place, the University of masters and scholars studying at Paris commends itself and its ready goodwill to please.

"That garden of delights, the University of Paris, the ancient mother and nurse of all studies, where the root of wisdom sends out its loftiest branches, where the tree of life unceasingly brings forth flowers and fruits of the graces, where also a living fountain issues, watering and fertilizing the whole globe of earth, to seek whose waters flock together the thirsty from every part of the world, and where whosoever wills may freely drink and be filled with the water of saving knowledge, has been wont rightly to commend to the various princes of the world and ecclesiastical prelates those accomplished men whom she has nourished and made perfect in divers sciences: and this the more zealously in proportion to the eminence of the degrees and position to which such persons have attained.

"Since, therefore, the reverend Doctor, Master John of St. German, your humble brother, and a venerable member of our body, by formal act a regent in Sacred Scripture; whose praiseworthy life, and nobility of proved virtue, and also the illustrious merits of his learning commend him; who for a long time has shone among us as a brilliant star without a stain; and who, by your favour which has in no small degree adorned our college, is preparing by your orders, as he says, to return to your parts; we with one accord and with all possible affection commend to your kindness this most lovable and beloved person.

"We beg you, if it please you, in accordance with the merit of his character, and with his position, and in consideration of our requests, so to treat him as to earn our thanks and favour, and to animate us all the more to honour others of your Order in the like circumstances. Be assured that whatever may be done, by you or by others, for this our master and venerated associate, that we shall count as done for our college.

"May the Most High long preserve you in prosperity and joy *in utriusque hominis statu*.

"Given at Paris in our general congregation at St. Maturin's, in the year of Our Lord, 1315, on the Sunday before the feast of the Nativity of St. John Baptist."

661

THE FORM OF COLLATION BY THE PRIOR, *SEDE VACANTE*, TO A VACANT BENEFICE IN THE GIFT OF THE BISHOP

Folio 67, d. No. 661. A.D. 1315

THE collation of Master John de Stratford, professor of civil law, to the church of Kempsey, was made on the 10th of the Kalends of July 1315, under this form of words:

"We, the Prior and Chapter of the cathedral church of Worcester, do appoint and provide Master John de Stratford, a man of prudence and discretion, to the church of Kempsey, with cure of souls, of the diocese of Worcester, belonging by proper right to the appointment, provision, and collation of the Bishop of Worcester for the time being, but for certain and lawful causes devolved on us and our chapter, and of our free goodwill confer on him that church with all its rights and appurtenances."

[This John de Stratford—for there were two—was the one who ultimately became Chancellor and Archbishop of Canterbury.]

668

A LETTER OF REQUEST ADDRESSED TO THE NEW ARCHBISHOP

Folio 68, d. No. 668. A.D. 1315

"To the reverend father, etc., the Lord Archbishop.

"Most loving father and lord, although when we were living under the rule of your piety, owing to the peace and protection we enjoyed from the first while you were our bishop and our defender, we had sufficient grounds supplied us for gratitude to God; yet now [*impresentiarum*] as is well understood through our brother John de St. Briavel, for the display of your goodness which you show so munificently towards our church, and towards ourselves to whom as to sons and pupils you offer advice and aid in our affairs, a stream of yet more abundant joy and exultation has flowed forth. That joy has been so great that we who as in duty bound used to pray for you, now making a virtue out of the necessity, with intense devotion, with diligent prayers and vows, are praying to God for you and for the welfare of the holy church, committed to your holiness and discretion at so stormy a time.

"We pray that He Who saved Peter from being drowned in the wave-tossed sea, He Who brought shipwrecked Paul safe to land from the depth of the ocean, may in like manner so assist you in the governance of His own ship, that under your guidance at the helm it may be guided and led to a haven of peace and prosperity in the Lord: and with our prayers we humbly offer to you such thanks as we can render for all the benefits you have conferred on us.

"But, dearest father, though whenever we shall be

in evils which we cannot evade we shall need your aid and favour, there is at present one intolerable burden we beg to be relieved from, which the bearer of these presents will in our name bring before your lordship, and we beg that if it please you you will grant him a favourable hearing.

" May the pre-eminence of your position and honour ever flourish and increase in the Lord."

A GLIMPSE INTO COUNTRY LIFE AND AMENITIES BETWEEN NEIGHBOURS AT MARTLEY

Folio 72, r. Nos. 698, 699. A.D. 1316

[In 698, 699 is a correspondence between Hugh le Despenser and the Prior in the year 1316 that throws light on the times. It is in old French, much of which would have puzzled me without the help of my learned friend, Madame Fautier.]

"To the good and wise man of Religion, Sire John, Prior of Worcester, Hugh le Despenser sends greeting.

"Sire, seeing that your servants and others of your service have cruelly hammered [*ledement demartele*], beaten, hurt, and grievously wounded my men to their great hurt and to our displeasure, we beg you to make redress for this misdoing; so that we and our said people may not have occasion to prosecute them in any other fashion. For we have heard that the majority of these men [*messesours*] are of your household and of your livery, and that since the event you have received and supported them. Which thing is to your danger: for some of those who were beaten were priests and clerks of the Mass.

"Wherefore it is good that you should look to the danger arising from it and the harm or damage that you may thereby incur. Be so kind as to let us know your answer by letter and by the bearer, what it shall please you to do in this matter. For know that we shall not leave the matter in peace without having secured satisfaction. God keep you.

"Written at Woking, June 15, 1316."

To this letter the Prior replies as follows:

"To the very honourable and wise lord, Hugh le

Despenser, his servant the Prior of Worcester, with honour and reverence.

"Very dear Sire,—As you have written by your letters that some of our household and others of our estate have cruelly set upon, beaten, hurt, and grievously injured your men to their great loss and to your displeasure, let your lordship be pleased to learn that such is not the case [*saver qe nient assint*]. But the dispute which arose between your men of Martley and our people was the fault of Martley, from what we have inquired and understood from the good country folk [*bones gentz de pais*]. For your men have killed some of ours, and others they have wounded nearly to death. Please to hear what is certain in this matter. And if hereafter we can discover that there was fault of our people in the jurisdiction of your lordship [*qe coupe ifuist de part de nos gentz en la ordinaunce de vostre seignurie*] who has been gracious to us in the present time, we will make honourable amends according to your will. God keep you."

704

THE FOUNDING OF A CHANTRY AT KEMPSEY

Folio 73, r. No. 704. A.D. 1316

OUR *Liber* gives us several examples in full detail of the founding of chantries. One, which I have described in my paper for the Worcester Historical Society, was at Elmley Castle, founded in 1310 by Guy de Beauchamp, Earl of Warwick, for no less than eight chaplains and four clerks. Another was at Kempsey, on a smaller scale, founded in 1316. I give an abstract of the deed of foundation, No. 704:

John of Kempsey, treasurer of the church of Hereford, under charter from King Edward II, and with the consent of John Deverrois, Rector of Kempsey, gives two messuages to God and the Blessed Virgin, mother of Christ, and to John Bromhale, presbyter, and his successor, for a Mass to be said daily at the altar of the parish church of Kempsey for his health [*salubri statu*] while he lived, and after his death for his soul, and the souls of his ancestors and benefactors, and the souls of all the faithful.

The messuages contain forty acres of land, of which the situation and boundaries are carefully described, furnishing many local names, both of places and persons. He grants also certain rents, payable in money, to supply wax candles to burn before the altar.

The presbyter, to be admitted to the chantry by the Bishop, shall take oath, touching the Holy Gospels, that faithfully, so far as the frailty of man's condition will permit, he will personally discharge the duty of the chantry, unless he is prevented by some irremediable or reasonable necessity, for which assertion the presbyter's word is to be believed. In that case he must arrange for some one else to perform his duty.

He is personally to be present, when he conveniently can be so [*quando commode poterit*] at mattins and the canonical hours; and he is subject to the visitation and correction of the rector as his ordinary, as other presbyters are of the same church. Moreover, the said presbyter shall say in the Mass one Collect with secret and post-communion for my health, and another Collect with secret and post-communion for my benefactors.

"Moreover, I desire that the presbyter who shall celebrate these Masses should live chastely and honestly to the praise of God and the honour of the glorious Virgin, and for the perpetual safety of his own soul. Should it happen, *quod absit*, that the presbyter after a first correction is charged with a second fall into sins of the flesh, and being convicted thereof does not or cannot lawfully purge himself, he must be deprived of the chantry by the ordinary, and another and fit presbyter appointed in his place. I ordain also that if the acting presbyter is at all suspected of incontinence with any woman, he shall avoid, under heavy penalty, ministering to that woman, and places that are under suspicion."

It is also ordered that at or on each succession the presbyter shall hand to his successor five marks' worth of crops or an equivalent in money. In these five marks' value are by no means to be reckoned the pot of brass, the tables, the forms, the trestles [*una olla enea, mense, formule, trestelli*] which he had given to John de Bromhale, nor the growing trees and grass.

Finally, he forbids any relative of his to interfere in any degree with this deed, which is signed and sealed by his own seal and those of the Treasurer of Hereford and the Bishop of Hereford, and is witnessed by many witnesses. The deed is dated Bosbury, February 4 (1316), in the ninth year of Edward II.

The tenor of the veritable Charter of our lord the King follows in these words:

"Edward, by the grace of God King of England, Lord of Ireland, and Duke of Aquitaine, to all to whom this letter shall come, greeting.

"Although by the common Council of our realm it has been ordered [*statutum*] that it is not lawful for men of religion or others to enter upon the freehold [*feodum*] of any one in such way that it may descend to the dead hand, without our consent and that of the lord-in-chief from whom mediately the property is held, nevertheless by means of a fine, which John of Kempsey has arranged with us, we have conceded and granted a licence, for ourselves and, as far as in us lies, for our heirs, that the said John shall be empowered to give two messuages, forty acres of land, two acres of meadow, and nine shillings and eight pence, value of rent, with their appurtenances in Kempsey, and assign them to a certain chaplain, who shall celebrate the Divine Service in the parish church of Kempsey, daily, for the soul of the said John, and the souls of his ancestors, heirs, and successors, to be had and held for ever by the said chaplain and his successors as chaplains who shall celebrate the Divine Service in the aforesaid church for the souls aforesaid.

"In like manner we have granted him a special licence, being unwilling that the said John or his heirs, or the said chaplain or his successors, should be disturbed or burdened in any respect, either by ourselves or our heirs, by reason of the statute aforesaid: saving, however, the due and customary services due from that estate to its lords-in-chief.

"In testimony whereof we have caused these letters patent to be made.

"Witnessed by myself, at Lincoln, on the 30th day of January, in the ninth year of our reign."

This is confirmed in the strictest way by the Bishop:

"Because we wish that this establishment shall in all its details in all circumstances remain firm and unshaken, we with diocesan authority canonically prohibit any one from infringing, hindering or disturbing this establishment and chantry, in any way, by any art or contrivance in the future, and we hereby excommunicate them.

"Bredon, June 11, 1316."

It is also finally confirmed by the Prior and Chapter, Worcester, June 22, 1316.

This is an interesting illustration of the steps to be taken in founding a chantry at that period, and of the way in which the Act of Mortmain was circumvented.

714

CORRODY GRANTED TO MASTER WILLIAM DE SCHOKERWYCH
(THEIR ARCHITECT)

Folio 76, r. No. 714. A.D. 1316

[This is an instance of the purchase of a corrody, or annuity for life.]

"LET all men know that we, John, Prior of the cathedral church of Worcester, and the chapter of the same place, have by our unanimous consent and of our mere goodwill, granted to our beloved in Christ, Master William de Schokerwych, architect [or master mason, *cementarius*], that he shall have and receive every day as long as he shall live, from our cellerar, one monk's loaf, and one white loaf of the old weight, and two gallons [*lagenæ*] of the best beer, and that he may once or twice in the week, as may seem to him convenient, apply for and receive the said beer at our brewery or cellar. He shall also receive from our kitchen on every flesh day a dish from the joint, with two dishes of pottage, such as a monk in the infirmary receives. And from the pittance what is called supper shall be that of two monks. On fish days he shall receive what is served from the kitchen to a monk in the refectory. All that he will receive from the kitchen will be brought to him by his servant in the kitchen."

"We have also granted to the same Master William that chamber in the tailor's shop which Nicholas of Norton, our fellow-monk, at one time occupied, and a stable there for one horse, with free entrance and exit, and whatever is necessary *familiæ suæ*.

"For this grant thus made to him the same Master

William has placed in our hands sixty pounds of silver.

" In testimony whereof we have caused our common seal to be appended to this deed.

" Given in our Chapter House at Worcester."

745

THE KING PLACES THE TEMPLARS' MANOR AT LAUGHERNE IN THE HANDS OF THE PRIOR

Folio 81, d. No. 745. A.D. 1309

[This document is out of its right place. It may have been in the possession of John de Wyke, and after his death copied into the *Liber*.]

" EDWARD, by the grace of God King of England, Lord of Ireland, and Duke of Aquitaine, to all freeholders and others on the manor of Lawarne [Laugherne], in the county of Worcester, greeting.

" Know that we have committed to our beloved in Christ, the Prior of Worcester, the aforesaid manor with its appurtenances, which belongs to the Master and brethren of the Knights of the Temple in England, and which for certain reasons is placed in our hands, for as long as we shall please, to be taken charge of, along with all the goods and chattels existing on our said manor. The Prior is to pay every year for the aforesaid manor whatever sum it shall be ascertained by a legal valuation made, or to be made, for that purpose that the manor is worth per annum ; one-half, that is to say, to our treasury at Easter, and the other half to our treasury at Michaelmas ; and he is to account at our pleasure for the aforesaid goods and chattels.

" And we, therefore, order you to acknowledge and answer to the same Prior, in the form aforesaid, as if he were our own prior, in all that concerns that guardianship of the manor and the goods and chattels aforesaid.

"In testimony whereof we have caused these our letters patent to be made.

"Witnessed by the Venerable Walter, Bishop of Worcester, our treasurer, at Westminster on the 27th day of January, in the second year of our reign (1309)."

746

MEMORANDUM OF THE FARM AT LAUGHERNE

Folio 81, d. No. 746. A.D. 1309

"MEMORANDUM that on the Saturday next after the feast of St. Valentine the Martyr, in the second year of the reign of King Edward, son of King Edward, the Sheriff [*vicecomes*] of Worcester, guardian of the manor of Lawarne, near Worcester, handed over to the Prior of Worcester, by a brief of our lord the King, the aforesaid manor of Lawarne, to be in his charge, along with all the goods and chattels existing in the same manor; to wit—

Ten oxen, value of each 8 shillings, total 4 pounds
Two cart horses, value of each 7 shillings, total 14 shillings
Three quarters of wheat, remnant left in the grange, price of each 4 shillings, total 12 shillings
Ten quarters of rye, remnant left in the grange, price of each 3 shillings, total 30 shillings
Twenty quarters of meal, *dragetum*, remnant in grange, price of each 2 shillings and 6 pence, total 50 shillings
Twenty-one quarters of oats, remnant in grange, price of each 20 pence, total 35 shillings
Two quarters of peas, remnant in the grange, price of each 2 shillings and 6 pence, total 5 shillings
A certain quantity of hay remaining, total 20 shillings
One bronze ewer, total 12 pence
Also forty acres of land sown with wheat, price of each acre 20 pence, total 66 shillings and 8 pence
Twenty-four acres sown with rye, price of each acre 16 pence, total 32 shillings

One cart in bad condition, bound with iron,
price 40 pence
Two ploughs with iron shares, total 2 shillings
The sum total of all the aforesaid goods and chattels,
17 pounds and 12 pence.

"In testimony whereof the aforesaid prior and deputy affixed their seals alternately to this indenture.

"Given at Lawarne on the day and year stated above."

749

A LETTER FROM ARCHBISHOP WINCHELSEY TO THE PRIOR CONCERNING THE ELECTION TO THE BISHOPRIC OF WORCESTER OF JOHN DE ST. GERMAN

Folios 82, 83 (inserted leaf). No. 749. A.D. 1303

[This is an important document, not known to exist elsewhere respecting the election of John de St. German to the bishopric of Worcester, which was approved by the King, and disallowed by the Pope, on the death of Godfrey Giffard. The document as it stands is obscure. Dr. R. L. Poole thinks that some words and even parts of sentences have been omitted ; he supplied those enclosed in brackets.]

" Robert, by Divine permission Archbishop of Canterbury, Primate of all England, to his beloved sons, the Prior and Chapter of the cathedral church of Worcester, salvation, grace, and blessing.

" Although at the visitation which we lately held at your convent we thought it right to charge the members of your chapter, all and each, in virtue of their obedience, under penalty of the greater excommunication, which we held over all who contravened our order, that no one of them, taking occasion by the visitation aforesaid, should presume to reproach another, or bring upon him any loss or annoyance or any accusation, yet nevertheless some of the brethren of the said chapter, swelling with ill-natured suspicions, are not afraid to take occasion of that visitation, as we have heard from a trustworthy person, to insult Gilbert the Sacrist and John the Cellerar, and daily to persecute them with words of reproach and contumely.

" They falsely and maliciously laid blame on them, asserting that they took occasion of visitation aforesaid [to the injury] of your house and its good name, to use the words of the calumniators. They asserted also that by sending letters to us and our clerks they [were able] to prevent our confirmation of the election of brother John Germeyn, whom you had really elected, when they ought conjointly with you to have specially supported.

" They [the monks in question] stated also that they [the Sacrist and Cellerar] to confirm their false statements, falsely invented the story that they had received [letters] from our clerks telling them that the confirmation of that election to be made by us was half written, and then on receipt of their letters was broken off.

" In fact, nothing of the sort happened or was thought of ; but long before our coming to you, without a suggestion [*excitatione*] from any one, we proposed to hold a visitation on account of the ill-health of your bishop, who was then living, with a view to the reformation of your monastery, and that of the whole diocese of Worcester.

" Such a visitation was called for on many grounds as necessary, and was evidently useful.

" The said election could not possibly on account of its defect, which was plainly brought to light, in defiance of the law, be confirmed.

" These monks have not only defamed their brethren, whom out of brotherly love they are bound rather to excuse even when to blame, by their false, malicious, and wicked slanders, but they have also seriously detracted from the good name and reputation of ourselves and our officials. It cannot then be doubted that they have by their fault incurred the sentence of greater excommunication, announced by us in the said visitation, and decreed by the holy fathers as the penalty for slanders of this sort.

"In order then that such wanton crime may not be the ruin of others by being left unpunished, we entrust the duty to you the Prior aforesaid, and in virtue of your obedience, and under threat of anathema we strictly enjoin and command you, that in the first place in our name by producing the true evidence you acquit the above-named [Sacrist and Cellerar] of all blame of this sort which has falsely been laid upon them; and then that you declare publicly to the brethren assembled in full chapter, that the aforesaid schismatical and contumelious slanderers, who have by the weapons of their malignity plotted to disturb and break up the unity of religious tranquillity, are excommunicate.

"After inquiring diligently as to their names, those whom you shall have found guilty of this false and malicious slander of their brethren and of ourselves you will specially declare to be excommunicated by our authority.

"And lest the whole of the Lord's flock be infected with their contagion, you will isolate them for a time from communion with their brethren under strict guard, until, after this wholesome chastisement of severe ecclesiastical discipline, when they have recovered their senses, they are fit to be sent to us, to receive canonically the benefit of absolution which we have kept in our own hands.

"We fear that it was with prophetic voice that we foretold you that by the obstinate vainglory and rash presumption of some of your rebellious brethren, which in various ways we noticed, your whole house, which may heaven avert, may be brought down into confusion and disgrace.

"Given at Walden, on the 10th Kalends of July, A.D. 1303, in the ninth year of our consecration (June 23, 1303)."

750

THE ACCOUNT OF THE CREATION OF A NEW PRIOR

Folio 83, r. No. 750. A.D. 1317

"*In nomine Dei. Amen.*" Thus begins a memorandum too long to quote in full.

After reciting the death of the late Prior, John de Wyke, on October 5, 1317, and his funeral on October 10, the public notary "John, called de Madeley, clerk, of the diocese of Worcester, public notary by the authority of the Holy Roman Empire," records with great detail and much repetition all the proceedings.

October 20 was fixed for the nomination, by the members of the convent, of seven of their own number, one of whom was to be selected by the Bishop to be the prior, in accordance with an agreement made between Bishop de Blois and the convent a century earlier.

Of the monks *one*, John of St. Germans, was absent, in Paris probably, and sent an apology. *Five*, Nicholas of Norton, Henry of Antioch, John of Pirie, Ralph of Scalleby, and Nicholas of Bertin, were in the infirmary, and sent word that they could take no part in the election. Forty-one were present; and judging from the latter half of the list, the names are arranged in order of admission to the monastery. The names are as follows:

Gilbert de Madeley, Sub-Prior.
Robert de Dickledisdone.
William de London.
John de Bruera.
5. William de Interberg.
John de Dumbeltone.
William de Wych.

Thomas de Chiltenham.
John de Harley.
10. John de Aston.
William de Bisseleye.
John de St. Briavel.
Richard de Bromwych, STP, Precentor.
Ranulph de Cathrop, STP.
15. Robert de Clifton, Cellarer.
William de Stanewaye.
Robert de Asserugge.
Marmaducus de Pirie.
Nicholas de Bradefield.
20. Adam de Cyrencestria.
Adam de Theukesbury.
John de Stratford, Almoner.
Simon le Botiler, Coquinarius.
Bogo le Bracy.
25. Henry Fouke, Sub-Sacrist.
Roger de Stevinton, Pitancer.
Simon de Defford.
Walter de Kereswelle.
William Nost.
30. Richard de Saltford.
Roger de Herwyntone.
John de Pedwardine.
Alexander de Brerhulle.
Wulstan de Branesforde.
35. Simon Crumpe, Notarius.
Richard de Winchcombe.
Nicholas Morice.
Robert de Morton.
John de Neuwyntone.
40. Roger de Henley.
William de Wykewane.

The Sub-Prior, Gilbert, appoints magister John de

Stratford [*quem ad hoc constituit organum suæ vocis*] to order all those monks, if there are any, who are disqualified by any cause for voting, to leave the Chapter House.

They then discuss "by what way they should proceed in the business of a nomination of this nature." At length they agree unanimously to proceed *per viam compromissi*; i.e. by delegation to a sub-committee whose choice of seven they agree beforehand that they will adopt.

The next step is to appoint this sub-committee of *nominatores*: and they appoint eight: Gilbert of Madeley, William of Wych, Richard of Bromwych, Ranulph of Cathrop, Robert of Clifton, Simon le Botiler, Henry Fouke and Roger of Stevyntone. These eight retired apart, and after discussing many names, as they afterwards stated, agreed on a list of seven, and appointed Robert of Clifton to announce the names to the convent.

This was done with every formality. "*In nomine domini Jesu Christi. Amen.*" The list was as follows:

John of Harleye.
Richard of Bromwych.
John of Stratford.
Simon le Botiler.
Henry Fouke.
Roger of Neuwyntone.
Wulstan of Bransford.

The next step is to appoint Robert of Clifton and Adam of Tewkesbury as their proctors to submit the list to the Bishop of Worcester, Thomas Cobham, and to request him "to deign to appoint one from those seven to be their prior."

They set forth, and "find the Bishop in the church of the hospital of the Blessed Mary Atte Strode," in the diocese of Rochester, and hand him the list of names. The Bishop desires more information; so they meet him on the following day in the parish church of Derceford, in the same diocese.

As the Bishop desires to be assured more fully on certain points [*de quibusdam amplius certiorari*] he delegates to Warin of Fulbourne, D.C.L., and Robert de Curton, two rectors in that diocese, to inquire by word of mouth as to the characters and qualifications of the seven.

This meeting is adjourned to the church of St. Dunstan in London. And then the Bishop, much pressed with business [*aliis arduis et inevitabilibus negotiis impeditus*], appoints James de Cobham, doctor of decrees, and Canon of Wells, to meet the proctors as his commissary with full power to select. He appoints Wulstan of Bransford in the following words, after a full rehearsal of the facts: "We, James de Cobham, special commissary of the aforesaid father for this business, by this present decree, appoint Wulstan de Bransford named above, whom the discipline of the monastic Order, ripeness of age, and proved weight of character make worthy of this gift of grace, willing, moreover, and able to defend the rights of his monastery alike in temporal and spiritual matters, one who has already enjoyed a foretaste of the church of Worcester, to be its Prior. In the name of Father, Son, and Holy Spirit."

The Bishop then wrote to the chapter announcing the appointment on November 23, 1317.

The witnesses were Robert de Valogne, Precentor of York Cathedral; Master John de Stratforde; Robert of Corton of Orwelle; Richard de Chadifle of Kemissey; William de Cornhulle of Aldismansbury; John de Madeley; and Robert de Luffenham, public notary.

On the same day, November 23, 1317, the Bishop orders the official of the Archdeacon to instal the Prior in the place which is his due, to induct him into all the rights and emoluments of the priorate, and to instruct the Convent to pay him canonical obedience.

On December 2 the official of the Archdeacon certifies the Bishop that he inducted the new Prior on November 30, that he instructed the monks and all others subject to the Prior as to their duty, and that there was no contradiction or opposition.

The Prior requests the Bishop's commissary to send him by the bearer a formal deed declaring his appointment as Prior, and to seal it with his own official seal, and the Bishop's seal; urging as the reason that his private seal is unknown to very many people [*quam pluribus est incognitum*]. He writes on the same subject to the notary public Robert de Luffenham: and repeats the request in a later letter.

766

A REQUEST MADE BY A CARDINAL-DEACON, AND THE PRIOR'S REPLY

Folio 85, d. Nos. 766, 767. A.D. 1317

" LUCAS, by Divine pity Cardinal-Deacon of St. Mary *in via lata*, to the men of religion the Prior and Convent of the church of Worcester, beloved by us in Christ, greeting in the Lord.

" Believing you to be lovers of piety and pity, we invite you with full confidence to a work of pity.

" Since John Rydel, son of Hugh Rydel, Knight, of the diocese of Lincoln, formerly Rector of the church of Torny, has now for some time past, on account of the war with the Scots, been unduly deprived of all the revenues and income of the aforesaid church, nor has any benefice from which in his poverty he can live honourably [*honeste*]; and since he hopes that through our intercession he will find with you timely favour to meet this deficiency, we exhort your charity, and beg you in the Lord, that you will receive this John, so commended to you, into your bowels of charity, and will provide him with sufficient necessaries at least until by God's consent [*Deo annuente*] peace is restored; when he can live, as he used to do, on the income of his said church. So listen to these our prayers that you may have merit in the sight of God, and that we may have good ground for commending your charity. Farewell. London, December 3, 1317."

767

THE PRIOR'S REPLY

" To the reverend father in Christ, the Lord Lucas, by Divine pity Cardinal-Deacon of St. Mary *in via lata*, his devoted sons, brother Wulstan, the humble Prior of the cathedral church of Worcester, and the Convent of the same place, reverence and honour as they commend themselves to him in due and devout subjection.

"We have just received your lordship's appeal on behalf of John Rydel, deacon, of the diocese of Lincoln, that we should be willing out of compassion to supply with all necessaries the said John, sometime Rector of the church of Torny, who has been despoiled of his church and all his goods by the Scots, at least until peace between the English and the Scots aforesaid shall have been restored.

"In truth, father and lord, although we are specially bound to works of piety, and although we greatly desire to respond to your appeal and precepts, nevertheless, fortune having been in many ways hostile to us and our predecessors, we have incurred such a load of debt, that though our daily allowance is diminished, we cannot meet our own needs. For these reasons we are unable, to our sorrow, to give effect to your lordship's appeal.

"We humbly pray you, therefore, on the ground of our inability to hold us excused.

"May the Most High preserve your paternity for ever, to His honour and to the advantage of the universal Church."

773

A TOUCH OF TENDERNESS AND PIETY

Folio 86, r. Nos. 773, 774. A.D. 1318

[A dear and faithful old monk of Worcester, John de Harley, who was admitted at the same time with the Prior, John de Wyke, had a young brother, Roger, who was a monk in Netley Priory. He had gone astray, and had been reclaimed by the Prior of Netley. Here are two letters from John de Harley; one to the good Prior of Netley, the other to his brother.]

"Long ago," he writes to the Prior, "father and revered lord, the kindness and humanity of God our Saviour appeared among us; when, not by works of righteousness which we have done, but according to His mercy, He saved us. Truly after the example of so great a Saviour, according to the parable which you have often read, you have in your own person placed on your shoulder the sheep wandering and lost, and have brought it back to the fold lest it perish; so that thus I and our other friends may speak of your recalling and reconciling brother Roger, our brother and your fellow-monk. Rejoice with me that I have found my sheep that was lost. He once took the habit in your sacred college, as you know: he put his hand to the plough, but looking back he went astray, doubtless like the sheep that was lost. Glad and rejoicing in all my heart at his recall, I offer you thanks, not such as I owe, but such as I can; humbly and devoutly entreating you, that now that he has been recalled by your kindness and care to the dwelling of the House of God, you will instruct him, as you know better than I, how to walk in the way of salvation; lavishing on him, if so it please you, the same counsel and favour."

[The following letter to his brother Roger was apparently sent with it.]

"Greeting: and may you know how sweet a thing it is to accept the Lord's yoke. You well know with how strong a chain Satan has bound you for many days. But now the Prince of Darkness in you has been conquered, that you may be for the future a child of light; and the Good Shepherd has placed on His shoulder the wandering sheep and brought it back to the fold. For this, with glad heart, I give thanks to the Father of Mercies, Who recalls and reconciles the wanderers. I earnestly pray you steadfastly to remain in the calling to which you have been called by the Lord's Will. May the Most High keep you for ever obedient to His most holy service.

[Such letters as these are naturally not often preserved. They show the existence of an undercurrent of feeling and piety in the convent, which finds no expression in the business documents which fill the book.

From Ann. Mon. iv. 480, we learn that Henry, lord of Harley, had six sons, who all became monks, at Worcester, Beaulieu, Hayles, Bordesley, Rufford, and Netley. John was the eldest brother, and Roger the youngest.]

780

A FORGIVENESS OF WRONGS, AND ADMISSION TO THE FRATERNITY

Folio 86, d. No. 780. A.D. 1318

"The Prior and Convent send greeting to their beloved clerk, William de Thorntoft, Rector of Dodderhill, who has requested to be admitted to their fraternity, and has written to seek pardon from us for any fault which he may have committed against our church or ourselves. We thank you for your services; and the stain of every fault with which you think your conscience may in any degree be burdened, by this letter of pardon, so far as lies in our power, we entirely abolish, and admit you to our fraternity."

784

THE PRIOR WRITES SAVAGELY AS A CREDITOR

Folio 86, d. No. 784. A.D. 1318

"To my disobedient son and perjured Vicar of Stanweye, Wulstan, Prior, etc., wishing for him the spirit of saner counsel.

"On the sight of these presents, send us without delay by the bearer that half-mark, for the withholding of which you are, as you know, perjured. But if you will have no regard to your pledge to us, broken to the peril of your soul, we cite you, the Vicar aforesaid, for the first, the second, and the third time in peremptory terms by this writing, to appear before the Lord Archbishop of Canterbury, on whose commission we rely, wherever he may be in his province or diocese, within fifteen days next following the date of this letter, to answer for perjury committed, and other charges to be brought against you in form of law, and further to do and to receive what justice shall decide.

"Given at Worcester, February 17, 1317/8."

793

THE PENANCE IMPOSED FOR STEALING FROM THE PRIOR'S WOODS

Folio 87, d. No. 793. A.D. 1318

"To John de Bradewas, a man of proved discretion, sequestrator to the reverend Lord Thomas (Cobham), Bishop of Worcester, Wulstan, Prior of the cathedral church of Worcester, greeting and the embrace of sincere affection.

"Those malefactors who cut down and carried off our timber, as you know, have appealed to you for remission of the sentence you thundered at them for their trespass. They have done so in spite of the fact that they had entered into an agreement with us as to the terms on which they could receive that remission. Lay on them, therefore, your injunctions as follows:

"Every one of the aforesaid malefactors, on the first Sunday in Lent, stripped to his shirt and barefooted, is to walk in our procession before High Mass, each carrying a wax candle, weighing one pound, and afterwards offer the candles at the great altar. You are to lay the same penance on the priest or priests, if there are any among them, with this exception, that out of reverence for the Order they may walk neither stripped nor barefoot. Let this, if you please, on no account be omitted. Farewell in Christ."

797

LICENCE TO CERTAIN MONKS TO PREACH AND HEAR CONFESSION

Folio 87, d. No. 797. A.D. 1317

"THOMAS (Cobham), by Divine permission Bishop of Worcester, to our beloved son the Prior of our cathedral church, greeting, grace, and blessing.

"The purer the seed sown in the Lord's field, and the more completely it is freed from noxious weeds by the labour of the husbandmen, the richer will be the fruits it brings forth. We, therefore, observing that some of your fellow-monks in the Lord's field are qualified, by their high character and their attainments in literature, for the office of preaching and hearing confessions, hereby license so to preach and hear confessions those whom you yourself, or whoever in our cathedral and outside it ordinarily provides for sermons, shall judge to be most suitable and honourable. We withhold from them, however, the power to absolve, except in cases in which absolution is permitted to parish priests; by no means intending to revoke the commission given through our Vicar-General to others of our penitentiaries to absolve in other cases.

"Given at London, March 17, A.D. 1318, and in the first year of our consecration."

801

PRIVATE TUITION: AND AN ATTEMPT TO SUPPRESS IT

Folio 88, r. No. 801. A.D. 1318

[This letter is of special interest to the historian of education in England.]

"To the man of venerable religion, by the grace of God Lord Prior of the cathedral church of Coventry, Wulstan, Prior of the cathedral church of Worcester, greeting, and wishes for success and happiness with ever-increasing honour.

"With confidence in your discretion we make special appeal to you on behalf of our beloved in Christ, James de Lyndeworthe, the instructor of the sons of T. de Whateleye.

"Master William de Wychebrook, *Rector scolarum* of Coventry, pleading the interest of his own scholars, is proposing, as we understand, on Wednesday next to involve him in a lawsuit and unjustly to harass him. James above-mentioned, at the instance of our beloved brother Richard de Bromwych, is teaching his cousins, as he may lawfully do, in their father's house. We entreat your reverence to give him your countenance and help in this matter; and to ask, and if it please you, warn him henceforth to desist altogether from the damaging calumnies which he is trying to bring upon him; to abandon for the future these citations and unjust vexations, and allow him to teach, as above described, his own pupils, as he has hitherto taught them.

"May the Most High ever preserve you in prosperity and honour."

826

THE BISHOP'S COMMISSION, AND A NUN'S PROFESSION

Folio 90, d. No. 826. A.D. 1318

[Bishop Cobham authorizes the Prior to receive the profession of the nuns of Whiston, the Whiteladies.]

"WE hereby entrust to you, the Prior of our cathedral church, the power to accept in our stead and with our authority, the profession of Sibilla de la Berewe, a nun of the monastery of Whiston, near Worcester, and all other nuns of the same monastery who desire to profess: the form of the rule of that religion, and all the canonical customs pertaining to that rule being duly and lawfully observed. In testimony whereof our seal is hereto annexed.

"Leicester, March 26, 1318, in the first year of our consecration."

The profession made by the nun was as follows:

"I, sister Sibilla, promise stability of purpose and conversion of character, and obedience, according to the rule of St. Benedict, before God and His saints, in this monastery built in honour of the Blessed Mary Magdalene. I do so in the presence of the venerable Wulstan, Lord Prior of the cathedral church of Worcester, the special commissary for this purpose of Thomas, by the grace of God Lord Bishop of Worcester, and of Alicia, Prioress of the aforesaid monastery. Having said this I have signed my name in the schedule containing my profession. Thus X X X."

829

A CARDINAL-DEACON'S DEMAND FOR HORSES

Folio 90, d. Nos. 829, 830. A.D. 1318

[This is a demand for conveyance, a post-warrant—*evectio*—enforced in the usual manner.]

"LUCAS, by Divine mercy Cardinal-Deacon of St. Mary *in via lata*, nuncio of the Apostolic See, to the man of religion the Prior, and the Convent of Worcester, greeting in the Lord.

"Since through various accidents we and our attendants have lately lost many of the horses which we had, and which were indispensable for our conveyance, engaged as we are in performance of business committed to us; and since in their place, for the carrying out the affairs now incumbent on us in the kingdom of England evections and other horses are necessary, we have decided to demand from you, by Apostolic authority, for one of our clerks, a horse and a suitable riding palfrey. It is in our power, and it is our duty to require these when expedient from ecclesiastical persons, seculars and regulars, exempt and non-exempt, as is more fully contained in Apostolical letters granted us for the purpose of requiring and receiving such evection; and we are ready wherever we may be to show you, if it is your wish, a copy with full attestations.

"Wherefore, by these presents, for the first, second and third time we peremptorily require and admonish you that within six days to be counted immediately following their receipt, of which we assign two for the first, two for the second, and the remaining two for the third peremptory command, no obstacle of any sort or difficulty or accident intervening, you shall cause the said evection or horse by some faithful messenger of your own, at your risk, however, and hazard and costs and expenses, to be granted and delivered with suitable saddle and bridle to our chamberlain.

"If, as we do not believe, you despise these our commands, we by the authority which we exercise in this matter, by this canonical monition sent in advance do from this time as if from then, hereby lay on you, the Prior, the sentence of excommunication, and on the Convent that of suspension, and we place your church under ecclesiastical interdict.

"We have as a precaution caused this letter, fortified with our seal, to be registered; and we repose entire trust in the bearer our sworn messenger.

"Given at Northampton on the 15th day of the month of July, in the 1318th year from the birth of Our Lord."

830

Receipt for the Same

"I, Bartholomew de Regio, Chamberlain of the reverend father Lucas, Cardinal-Deacon of St. Mary *in via lata*, nuncio of the Apostolic See, acknowledge that I, in the name of the said Lord Cardinal, have received from the Prior and Convent of Worcester, desirous to obey the letters of the said Lord Cardinal within the period stated in the said letters, one white horse with saddle and bridle. In testimony whereof I give this letter signed with my seal.

"Given at Erwahaton, August 8, 1318."

834

SOME CORRESPONDENCE BETWEEN THE PRIOR OF WORCESTER AND THE ABBOT OF RAMSEY

Folio 91. Nos. 834–839. A.D. 1318

There is some remarkable and rather heated correspondence between the Prior of Worcester and the Abbot of Ramsey in the year 1318 respecting the return to Worcester of one of their monks, Ranulph de Cathrop, who had been lent to Ramsey as a lecturer on Scripture. The correspondence occupies documents 834 to 839; it is partly undated; in one case perhaps wrongly dated, and some letters are missing; but the tenor of it is clear.

The Prior, Wulstan of Bransford, reminds the Abbot (834) that Ranulph was lent them only for a time, and might be recalled at the Prior's pleasure; and tells him that it is now necessary for certain reasons to recall him. He further requests the Abbot to provide a carriage for him; explaining that in consequence of the late vacancy in the priorate, the Pope's collector of first-fruits had sequestrated everything they possessed, "so that they dared not lay a hand on a carriage or anything else."

He encloses a letter to Ranulph from the chaplain, ordering him to return forthwith.

The Abbot replies courteously (835) on December 19, 1318, that he regrets that, in consequence of the Cardinal's post-warrants [*evectiones*] and the absence of his carriages at York for the Parliament, he is unable to send a carriage. No blame must be attached to Ranulph, as he wished to return. He relies on the Prior's goodness. He regrets that the chaplain wrote so imperatively—*minus modeste quam debuit ad tantum virum.* He hopes Ranulph will return to Ramsey some day.

Ranulph's own reply is not given. But the Prior replies angrily, not to say rudely (836).

"We have received your letter giving the reason for Ranulph's delay, which out of respect for you we would accept if it were adequate, and in agreement with his own. He could unquestionably have hired a carriage in Ramsey. We wish you to know that we ratify all our chaplain said: we do not hold Ranulph to be so great a man. As to your request, we will gladly send him back when all that can be done in our monastery for our convenience and honour is complete."

A second letter is written to Ranulph. They had ordered him to return at once, to take the place as *lector* which Richard de Bromwych had vacated at the order of the presidents to visit other convents, and he had not obeyed. They now order him to return at once, and to preclude excuses [*ut viam excusationes frustratorias allegandi de certo precludamus*] they send a carriage.

The Abbot keeps his temper and sends Ranulph back, but writes a dignified remonstrance. This is 837, also dated December 19.

"When he recalls the warm friendship that ought to bind churches together he is surprised that the request from Ramsey, granted by the late Prior, should be set aside by others animated by a different spirit. Most men think that Worcester is more bound to help the monastery of Ramsey than one of Saint Augustine. God knows we desired Ranulph for the honour of God and of our Order; and we have no one else. We adjure you [*obsecramus in domino*] to send him back. It will be for the honour of both churches. If you refuse, it will lead to strained relations between us which we ought to avert."

The Prior does not return a soft answer (838).

"He wonders that the recall of Ranulph should surprise the Abbot. One who has gathered the flowers of learning and virtue from his own monastery is bound to refresh the hearts of his brethren with their fragrance: nor does it seem surprising that an unjustifiable request, with all respect for him who makes the request, should fail.

"As to your imputation that we are 'animated by a different spirit,' we assure you that it was from zeal and the Spirit of God leading us that we all assented to it. We also, according to our measure, have a zeal for our Order. But zeal, like charity, may begin at home [*poterit a seipso sicut et caritas incipere*].

"On these grounds we cannot send our brother back. We do not take your unwise hint that we should fear the sting of the threat contained in your letter. Our marvel is that where we should have received thanks, we only meet with indignation and threats."

This closes the correspondence, interesting and valuable on several grounds; but not quite creditable to our Prior.

It may be noted that Ranulph was selected in 1304 by Bishop Gainsborough as a promising scholar and sent to Oxford partly at the Bishop's expense. He took his degree with much honour in 1312.

Worcester, it will be remembered, had close links with Ramsey. Both looked to St. Oswald as their founder, and the first Prior of Worcester, Wynsin, was trained at Ramsey.

844

AN INVITATION FROM PRIOR WULSTAN TO A FRIEND

Folio 92, r. No. 844. A.D. 1318

"To his confidential friend, A. de H., Wulstan, Prior of the cathedral church of Worcester, greeting.

"We by this letter specially beg and urge you, as a friend in whom we have full confidence, that you will come to us at Worcester for Christmas, which is now close at hand; and that you will stay with us a few days, dining at our table in this festal season, and thus at once gratify and honour us.

"Be assured that we cannot bear with equanimity the thought of your absence at that feast.

"Please to assure us by the bearer that you will come."

[The invited guest is perhaps Adam of Horwyntone, a commissary of Adam Orlton, Bishop of Hereford.]

848

HOW DID MONKS APPOINTED BY THE BENEDICTINE GENERAL CHAPTER AS VISITORS OF MONASTERIES TRAVEL?

Folio 92, r. No. 848. A.D. 1318

A LETTER from Richard de Bromwych throws light on this. He had been appointed by the General Chapter of Benedictines in the province of Canterbury to be a visitor of Benedictine houses. It would seem that it was expected that he should travel at the cost of his own convent; but he demurred, in the following letter:

"To the Abbots of C. and W. [probably Chertsey and Walden], Presidents of the General Chapter of the Order of St. Benedict in the province of Canterbury, brother R. de B. [Richard de Bromwich], a humble monk of the cathedral church of Worcester.

"Though I am ready in due obedience to discharge to the best of my power the commission you have laid upon me, yet in conjunction with the Prior I hereby request that, for reasons laid before you by the Prior, you will altogether hold him excused from supplying me with a carriage and other necessaries for the office of visitation; and that you should write to other heads of houses, and lay it on them to provide me with carriages, and other necessaries."

849

MONASTERIES CONFER AS TO AN IMPENDING VISITATION

Folio 92, d. Nos. 849–857. A.D. 1318, 1319

LETTERS 849–857, written in the winter of 1318–1319, throw some light on the triennial visitations of Benedictine houses in the province of Canterbury, and on the co-operation of the convents. None of the letters are dated; and they are plainly not entered in chronological order.

In 849 the Prior writes to the Abbot of St. Peter's, Gloucester, that he understands that on the receipt of a mandate from the visitors of the monasteries of Gloucester, Evesham, and Worcester, appointed by the General Chapter, he consulted his clerks on some doubtful points. The Prior would wish to take the same line, and asks the Abbot to send him information by the bearer. "Many of us," he writes, "think that the mandate is discreditable to the Presidents; and are of opinion that a message should be sent to one or both of them, asking them to defer the visitation till the next General Chapter. Will the Abbot kindly give his advice?"

In 854 he writes to the Abbot of Evesham, wishing to consult him as to joint action: and encloses copy of a letter he has sent to Gloucester pointing out the legal flaw in the appointment of the visitors. They ought to be appointed in chapter [*debent in capitulo deputari*], but they were not: *de illis asserentibus se visitatores nulla fit mentio.*

In 850 we have the reply from Gloucester. The Abbot consulted John de Stratford—the clerk to the King who was afterwards Archbishop of Canterbury—and he sends his opinion to the effect that the Presidents have exceeded their powers; that there is, therefore, ground for appeal. But in order to avoid a row [*pro briga in hac parte vitanda*] it is better not to resist; it would create a disturbance; we are unlikely to get better visitors; and we shall get no good, but only blame. He advises writing to the visitors to ask them to delay their visitation till after the feast of the Purification (February 21), on account of the absence of some brethren. "We are prepared," he continues, "to send to the Presidents, in conjunction with you and the Abbot of Evesham, our view of the errors of the commission; and if they do not yield, we should admit the visitors after protest."

This is very sane and sound advice.

In 852 the Prior writes to Ralph of London, Prior of Shrewsbury, as John de Stratford advises; but he only asks him to visit Worcester last instead of first in his group [*nos nunc primos velitis ordinare postremos*]. And in 853 the Prior consents to this, and names January 26; and this is reported in 851 to Gloucester.

In 855 the Abbot of Evesham thanks the Prior of Worcester, and adds other reasons why the visitation should be postponed. "The Earls of Arundel and of Pembroke, and Hugh Despenser and his son and others, will be meeting at Worcester and in his own neighbourhood in that week, and the disturbance would interfere with the office of a visitation. We think," he writes, "that before spring approaches we should at once send a joint request to the Prior of Shrewsbury to postpone his coming until we have consulted the Presidents, as on the grounds you urge we have not decided to admit the visitors, and we ask him further to communicate this to his colleague. We do not wish to show any disrespect to the Presidents or visitors, and meantime we shall consult one of the Presidents."

In 856 the Prior tells the Abbot of Evesham that the Worcester visitation has been postponed, and that he does not doubt that he will obtain a similar postponement: and from 857 we learn that the Evesham visitation was put off to Mid-Lent Sunday.

865

THE POPE'S TENTH COLLECTED IN THE DIOCESE OF WORCESTER

Folio 94, r. No. 865. A.D. 1318

[Occasionally among the other documents in the *Liber Albus* are accounts for money received and transmitted.]

"THE account of the Prior and Convent of Worcester, appointed sub-collectors in the diocese of Worcester of the yearly tenth imposed on the clergy of England by the most holy father, John XXII, by Divine Providence the Lord Pope, rendered by brother John de St. Briavel, a monk of Worcester, proctor for the said Prior and Convent, in presence of John of Cokermuthe and John of Malmesbury, special commissaries of the venerable father John, by the grace of God Lord Bishop of Winchester, chief collector of the said tenth in this region, in the hospice of the said father at Southwark on the Monday next after the octave of St. Hilary, A.D. 1318."

An abstract of the account is as follows:

	£	s.	d.	£	s.	d.
The total tenth of ecclesiastical income is				736	5	10¼
Of this the following sums have already been paid:						
To Robert Person	246	5	9			
„ Bertrand del Muyr and the merchants of Gascony . .	374	0	0			
„ King's Exchequer . . .	20	0	0			
				640	5	9
Leaving a balance of .				96	0	1¼

From this they request remissions as follows :

	£	s.	d.	
For poor hospitals and nuns, mendicants and churches rated at 6 marks, or less . . .	11	14	2¾	
For the Bishop's property in the diocese	48	11	3½	
Subsequently paid to Arnold Forspere	20	0	0	
Allowed to hospitals . . .	2	3	0	
Paid at the audit . . .	5	2	11½	
Expenses of collection . .	8	0	0	
Balance still owing . . .		7	7½	
				95 19 1¼

For this account the Bishop of Winchester gave them a receipt dated April 28, 1318. *Quieti estis de illo. Approbamus omnem executionem.*

871

THE INCOME OF A VICARAGE APPROPRIATED TO AN ALIEN MONASTERY

Folio 95, r. No. 871. A.D. 1316

THIS is a long document, and is of considerable interest, both as showing the miscellaneous sources of income of a Vicar, how an alien convent to which the church was appropriated cut that small income down, and how the Bishop forced them to increase it.

The church of Astley was appropriated to the monastery of St. Taurin, at Evreux, in Normandy. A complaint reaches Bishop Walter Maidstone that the Vicar's income is being cut down unduly. He, therefore, appoints a strong commission to inquire and report.

They report that "William, perpetual Curate of Astley, and his predecessors as far back as is known, have had the manse and curtilage and gardens and land attached to the manse, and all the offerings at the altar. Also from the Convent and Church the Vicar has received five quarters of wheat, five of rye, ten of barley, and ten of oats at the hands of the Prior of Astley; and also tenths of the hay from all the parish, except four named meadows which supplied one cartload; also two cartloads of their barley at Astley, and the tithe of a dovecot at Astley, and of all the gardens and curtilages of the whole parish, except the ancient demesnes, and free access to a spring of water below his garden. Also *duo averia scilicet boves vel vaccas cum averiis*, besides common pasturage, six pigs, and six cartloads of firewood from the woods of the demesne."

They find that this provision is too small; and

that though it is so the Convent and Prior have still further diminished it—*ita quod ipsam vicariam intollerabiliter reddunt exilem.* The document specifies what has been withheld, *in animarum vestrarum periculum et aliorum perniciosum exemplum*, and threatens legal proceedings lest the vicarage *ad desolationem perpetuam deducatur.*

The whole question is examined again in Worcester Cathedral before another commissary of the Bishop, the Vicar appearing in person, and the Convent by a proctor, and the commissary decides that the income is to revert *ad pristinum statum quo fuerat*—to what it had originally been.

872

THE PAINTED CHAMBER IN THE PRIORY GRANTED TO AN HONOURED CORRODY HOLDER

Folio 96, r. No. 872. A.D. 1319

Some of the documents incidentally give us information as to the buildings. In this we see that there was a Guesten Hall before Wulstan of Bransford built the splendid hall of which part still exists; and that near it was a painted room which it was a special honour for a guest to occupy.

"Let all men whom this writing reaches know that we, brother Wulstan, Prior of the cathedral church of Worcester, and the convent of the same place, have granted for ourselves and our successors, to our beloved and faithful clerk, Master John of Bitterley, as long as he shall live, in our priory at Worcester, with free entrance and exit, that chamber which is called the Painted Chamber, near the Hall of Guests, with free use of the same for his convenience and honour.

"In testimony whereof our common seal is appended.

"Given in our chapter house at Worcester, on the 8th of the Ides of August (August 6), A.D. 1319."

887

LEAVE GIVEN TO A MONK TO ACCEPT THE PRIORATE OF ANOTHER MONASTERY

Folio 98, r. No. 887. A.D. 1320

"LET all men know that we, Wulstan, Prior of the cathedral church of Worcester, moved by the prayers of the venerable fathers John, by the grace of God Lord Bishop of Llandaff, and Adam, by the same grace Lord Bishop of Hereford, and also of the noble Lord John of Hastings, Lord of Abergavenny, and favourably inclined to thee our brother Richard de Bromwych, a monk of our own, when you request licence to consent to your provision to the rule of the priory of the Blessed Mary of Abergavenny by the venerable father, Lord Adam of Hereford aforesaid, who has, as is asserted, sufficient authority in this matter, and licence to migrate thither, on the ground that you desire, as we believe, to win fruits of grace in the Church of God; we, therefore, do, by these presents, grant to thee, brother Richard aforesaid, licence to consent to the provision made for thee, and to migrate to the said priory, and to remain there continually; absolving thee from all obedience owing to us, and setting thee free from us and our successors.

"In witness of this request and permission, we desire that one part of this indenture under our seal shall be retained by thee, and the other part under the seal of the Abbot of Pershore by us in our church of Worcester.

"Given and done, as to us, the Prior of Worcester, in our priory on the 4th day of October, in the year of Our Lord, 1320; and also signed by us, the Abbot of Pershore, aforesaid, on the 18th day of October, in the year stated above."

Note.—From 1082, it appears that the Convent recalled him in 1325, to teach Scripture at Worcester.

892

THE POSITION, PRIVILEGES, AND PENSION OF THE CHIEF PORTER

Folio 99, r. No. 892. A.D. 1320

[The following indenture, dated October 19, 1320, throws some light on life in college, and on other points.]

"THE Prior and Convent grant to Warin Giffard of Coldicote daily for life one monk's loaf, and one gyst of the best beer, and from the kitchen the allowance of a prior's esquire [*armiger*] and an armiger's fur robe. He has the porter's chamber, and a stable and hay for one horse, and the post of chief porter [*janitor*] for life, with the usual stipend [*feodus*] and a servant, to be appointed and dismissed at his own pleasure, to be paid as usual by the Prior and Convent."

Whenever he leaves the town on business of the Convent they pay his expenses, and the allowance lapses; if on his own business it lapses till his return. If he returns at any hour before curfew [*piritegium*] he receives the day's allowance.

Warin takes the oath of faithful and diligent service to the Convent. He will also, if requested, attend on the Lord Prior as his marshal, whenever he dines elsewhere than in the refectory or *misericordia*. If owing to ill-health he cannot perform his duties, he nevertheless retains his position and privileges; and they grant him another servant to wait on him, who will receive from the cellerar a loaf which is called a pricket loaf, and a pottle [*potellum*] of servant's beer, to be stopped if he is absent for any reason. When he returns, the same arrangement to hold as above.

For all these things Warin gives twenty-five pounds of silver into the hands of the Prior and Convent.

906

LOCAL NAMES OF FARMS AND HOLDINGS PRESERVED

Folio 100, d. No. 906. A.D. 1321

THE local historian of parishes will find some local names of places and farms and holdings are preserved in documents in the *Liber Albus*. One specimen shall be given.

"The Prior and Convent of Worcester in 1321," for no reason assigned, "grant to Hugh the Prior, and the Convent of Great Malvern, all their lands and tenements, with the gardens, curtilages, meadows, fields, pastures, woods, moors, plains, roads, paths, hedges, ditches, and all and each of their belongings which we had and held in Powick, Bransford, and Leye"—only the names, not the descriptions, are given here—"Gildhalle, Langefurlong, Poulecroft, Coulecroft, Arlehey, Neweland, Marhull, Delefield, Warchya, Wyglinghale, Redehedle, Wyginhale, Brademewe."

Some of these names may still survive in those three parishes.

935

THE CONVENT AND ITS SUPPLIES TO THE KING'S ARMS

Folio 104, r. Nos. 935–939. A.D. 1321

An interesting historical section might be compiled from these letters, and I have given an abstract of them in my paper to the Worcester Historical Society. But I add here the latest correspondence that I have reached.

In December 1321 the King writes (935) to the Prior that he is compelled, by business closely affecting the Church and the realm, to send forces to the Welsh Marches; and asks him to furnish from his people as many strong fighting men as he can, and to send them well mounted and equipped by the 20th of the month, to be for a time at the Prior's cost, and then at the King's; and to let him know at once how many he will send, and how long he will support them.

The Prior replies (936) "that we cannot find men-at-arms [*gentz d'armes*] in these parts who would go, for anything that man could give or promise them, either to the Marches or the other great movements in your land." He, therefore, begs to be excused.

The King writes again (937) on February 1, 1322, that "before our coming to your house we entreated you by letter to assist us in our great need, and you have done nothing." He urgently renews his request.

This is the only reference I have met with to any visit of Edward II to the priory.

The Prior again pleads inability (938), and sends to the King, who is at Hereford, one of the monks, Robert de Morton, to give further verbal explanations. They send by him a letter of credence (939), as follows.

I give a very literal translation, and also a specimen of the original text. As will be seen it is not free from difficulties, and experts whom I have consulted are not in agreement as to the meaning of some of the words. The MS. is perfectly legible.

"Very dear and much-loved lord. Your humble chaplains, the Prior and the Convent of Worcester—to whom lately you have twice written, and have once by your servants commanded that they should render you aid for your great needs and weighty enterprises, which may God in His pity guide to His honour and to the safety of yourself and of your people—by me, their brother, if it please you, give you to understand that at all times they have been, they are, and they will be of ready will to accomplish your desire, as far as they can. But since their property in common with that of others in the realm is depressed by pestilence and deaths which have come to pass, and in particular, more than all others in the kingdom,* by the men of might who have come from the Marches and the long stays with them for all this year, and now worse than all this by the coming of the magnates who have lately made perquisitions in Worcester and have left nothing in the country. They pray and urge you, for the love of God, that you, having regard to the matters aforesaid, and to the distress and want which they suffer in eating and drinking and other necessities, will deign to hold our will free from blame, and excused by reason of our inability to carry out your order."

"Mes pur ce que lour estat communement od autres du roialme est abese par pestilences et mortalites escheues et especialment outre toutz ceux du roialme par les soverneles venues de marcheis et longes

* Perhaps "the frequent comings from the Marches."

demeores od eux a tote ceste anee et ore a pir de tout par la venue des grands qore dreint Wirecestre pristrent ne rien en pais linquerent. Vous prient et requerount par amour de dieu que vous eiauntz regard a choses dites et a la destresse et defaute en manger beivre e autres necessites deignez avoir lour volonte de blame e par noun poer de vostre maundement faire excuse."

[No letter that I have yet come to shows so vividly the disorganization and distress of the country at that time.]

940

HOW THE CONVENT RAISED MONEY BY MORTGAGING THE FUTURE

Folio 104, d. No. 940. A.D. 1321

In 940 the Convent made an agreement with one William of Cirencester, a chaplain, of a singular kind. He paid them 20 marks down, for which they gave him a monk's allowance of bread, meat, pottage, and beer for life: but William also promises that, as long as he lives and is able to do so, he will "celebrate" daily in the cathedral in such manner and places, and for such persons as the Prior and Convent shall direct [*celebrabit diatim taliter qualiter ubi et pro quibus indictum fuerit*]. This was dated December 21, 1321.

In 941, on February 7, 1322, they raise 20 marks more in ready money, and pledge themselves to supply Robert de Boys with food, and a suitable dwelling in the city [*domicilium sibi competens in villa*].

On May 16, 1322, they raise £40 ready money, a sum at least equivalent to £600 to-day, from Peter de Greet, clerk, a citizen of Worcester; and they employ him also as their rent collector in the city. He swears on the Holy Gospels that from that hour he will be faithful to the cathedral church, to Wulstan the Prior, and the Convent, their successors, and honestly account for all rents collected by him or any other for whom he binds himself to answer [*dum sanus fuero et senio non confractus*]. He also swears that he will do his utmost to protect the interests of the church and all its dependents [*familiares et nativi*] in the city and for a mile outside; that if anything dangerous to their interests comes to his knowledge he will protect them ; or, if he cannot do so, he will warn them ; and that he will reveal their secrets, or anything to their discredit, to no living creature [*nulli viventium*].

In return for all this cash and service they promise him daily for his life, for himself and his mother Isabella, one monk's loaf of the weight known as St. Wulstan's, one gallon of good beer, one servant's loaf, and one gallon of servant's beer ; and if he dies before his mother they will continue to her the servant's loaf and beer.

Thus the Bursar raised cash, but burdened the future.

951

CONNEXIONS BETWEEN MERTON COLLEGE, OXFORD, AND WORCESTER PRIORY

Folio 106, d. No. 951. A.D. 1322

THE relations between our Convent of Benedictines and a definitely secular foundation like that of Merton College are of special interest.

In A.D. 1322, Bishop Thomas Cobham writes:

"The late Walter de Merton, sometime Chancellor of the illustrious Lord Henry, King of England, founded and established, for the honour of the Divine Name and the perpetual advantage of the most holy Church, a house which is called the house of the Scholars of Merton, in his manor of Mandone, in the diocese of Winchester, for the perpetual support of scholars attending the school, and of the ministers of Christ's altar residing in the said house. We, awaiting the fruit which by God's mercy we hope and believe will herefrom for ever accrue to the Church of God to the worship of the Christian religion, after first holding diligent and solemn inquiry along with our chapter, and with their expressed consent, do, in the name of the Holy and Undivided Trinity, grant and assign and appropriate to their own use the church of Wolvorde of our diocese, along with its chapels and all its rights and appurtenances, in which the said scholars and brethren, by the collation of the men of religion the Prior and Convent of Stanes, of the diocese of Coventry and Lichfield, hold the right of patronage [*jus obtinent patronatus*] for the relief of their poverty, and the increase of their number, in which we see the manifest advantage of the Christian religion.

"We ordain that they shall hold and possess it for the said uses as soon as it shall be vacant; and that it is lawful for them on the authority of these presents to enter the Church, and to possess it in peace with all its rights and appurtenances when it becomes vacant."

The deed closes as usual with the claim to fix the Vicar's stipend, and of increasing or diminishing it as circumstances require [*juxta temporum qualitates*]; and with reserving all rights of bishop, cathedral, and archdeacon, and is dated July 13, 1322. Stanes is Stone, in Staffordshire, and Wolvorde is Wolford.

The house of "The Scholars of Merton" was founded by Walter de Merton at Malden, in Surrey, in 1264. See *Dict. Nat. Biog.* His epitaph is quoted there: *Re, unius exemplo, omnium quotquot exstant collegiorum fundator.*

In the June of the year following, 1323, the Warden and Scholars and Brethren of Merton College, Oxford, send a deputation to the Prior and Convent of Worcester with the following letter (No. 968):

"To the venerable father in Christ the Lord Prior of Worcester, and the reverend Convent of the same place, their humble and devoted servants, the Warden of the House of Scholars of Merton, in Oxford, the Scholars and Brethren of the same house, send their reverence and honour, with every desire to please.

"We naturally cannot forget with what sweetness of charity, and with what gifts of liberality, you have hitherto followed us as if we were your own. The more attentively we study your kindness, the sweeter does it become in our regard. Considering then your lordship as so favourably inclined towards us, from the depth of our hearts, as far as our small powers permit, we return to each and all of you the fullest expression of our thanks.

" Taking then from the past confidence as to the future, with our earnest prayers we urge and entreat your benevolence that to our beloved Master Richard de Cameshale, professor of sacred scripture, and to John de Aischtone, fellows of our house, in those matters which, speaking for us, they will bring before your lordship, the wonted clemency of your piety will deign to grant a kind audience and undoubting trust, and that to the prayers which, through these our messengers, we pour out to you, you will open wide the channels of the fountain of your grace and favour *ut qui in subrogatione in domo nostra facienda de Wigorniensi diocesi scolares assumpsimus de gratia speciali nostrarum precum pia exauditione ad sumendum habiles astringamur sicut in aliis dioscesibus in quibus beneficia nostro consistunt victui deputata vinculo sacramenti.*

" May the Lord Jesus Christ vouchsafe to guide you happily for many years in the keeping of His commandments.

" Written at Oxford, June 14 (1323)."

The passage in Latin may be translated : " That we who in filling vacancies in our house have by special favour admitted scholars from the diocese of Worcester may be bound by oath, on your kindly acceptance of our prayers, to admit competent persons, as in the case of other dioceses in which are benefices appropriated to our maintenance."

It seems to be a proposal to appropriate some scholarships at Merton to candidates from the diocese of Worcester. Dean Rashdall writes that Statute 14 orders that any one who enters religion ceases to belong to the college. Hence the consent of the monastery was asked for, not because it concerned their monks going to Oxford, but as the Chapter for the Bishop and the diocese generally.

On folio 46 (*b*) of the *Liber Eccl. Wig.* (Worc. Hist. Soc., 1912) is contained a letter from Archbishop Walter requesting the Chapter to confirm the appropriation of the church of Wolford to the Scholars of the House of Merton, whom he describes as *mundanis abjectis illecebris in studio continuo litterarum laudabiliter insudantes, et demum domino dirigente ad altiora vocati in dei ecclesia fructus uberiores producentes.*

955

THE ARCHBISHOP SUMMONS CONVOCATION IN THE PERILS OF THE INVASION BY THE SCOTS

Folio 107, r. No. 955. December 2, A.D. 1322

THE following is an abstract:

The Archbishop describes at length the urgent perils of the time from the invasions by the Scots and their accomplices; how at this time with a large army of warriors they have invaded the greater part of England, and have savagely depopulated and laid waste nearly the whole of it, killing all without regarding condition, rank, sex, or age; spoiling, robbing and burning houses, castles, towns, churches, and monasteries. He knows that the clergy are themselves weary; but at the prayers of the King and the demands of the people, he must convoke them.

He summons his fellow-bishops, and suffragans, deans and priors of cathedrals, archdeacons, abbots, and priors of other convents, *per se regentes*, and proctors for the clergy, to come to Lincoln on the day after St. Hilary (January 14). He insists on their presence. "We do not intend as hitherto to spare those who are absent and do not take the trouble to attend; but we shall proceed against them and punish them with the utmost rigour of the law [*quatenus de jure permittitur*]. Things which concern all should be approved by all; and in this case the necessity is manifest and unprecedented, the danger urgent, and demand the prompt consideration of all.

"Lincoln, December 2, 1322."

971

THE ACT OF MORTMAIN CIRCUMVENTED

Folio 109, d. No. 971. A.D. 1323

[The Prior and Convent confirm a deed by the Bishop, which appears to circumvent the act of Mortmain. The Bishop's deed is as follows :]

" ALTHOUGH by the common council of the kingdom of England it has been decided that it is not lawful for the religious or others to acquire any fief [*feodum*] so that it passes to the dead hand without the licence and will of the King and the Lord-in-Chief from whom the property is immediately held, yet we, from our special devotion to the glorious Virgin Mary, in whose honour the abbey of Evesham is founded, and from our great affection for the abbey and the persons in it, and to increase Divine worship therein, grant to Hawysia of Gloucester leave to give to the Abbot and Convent of Evesham the manor of Tatlinton, which she holds from us, with all that pertains to it ; and we grant leave to the Abbot and Convent to receive and hold it.

" Hartlebury, April 2, 1323.

" Confirmed in chapter, April 3, 1323."

On May 12, 1323, the King granted a licence for the gift of this manor to Evesham, *cf.* Calendar of Patent Rolls, 1321–1324, p. 285.

1008

A TESTIMONIAL FOR A CANDIDATE FOR ADMISSION TO THE MONASTERY

Folio 113, d. No. 1008. A.D. 1323

"BROTHER John of Worcester, Monk of Glastonbury, and Precentor, to the most holy Prior and Convent of Worcester, greeting.

"I thank you, my Lord Prior and reverend father, that it hath pleased you to send me your fatherly letter, and to make trial of my humble services and reverence.

"In that letter you have signified to me that you would be glad to receive Robert de Weston as a monk, seeing that he is commended for his learning and his character, had you not heard, somewhat doubtfully, that he comes of servile stock [*de servili genere*]. It is this doubt that you wish should be cleared up by my answer, addressed to yourself and the Convent jointly; and that the clerk should himself be sent with my letter of testimonial, should I, after diligent examination, think him worthy to be admitted among you.

"Your most blessed meeting may know certainly that the father of the said clerk holds land under our Abbot in Weston, and that it is free land, not serf [*liberam non nativam*]. This fact is attested and asserted by the joint evidence of the cellerar of our house, the bailiff of the place, and other trustworthy persons who know. He possesses a creditable knowledge of letters [*literaturam laudabilem*] and is commended by our Master Edmund, and the scholar-monks now in our house. By the process of learning he will know more of song than he knows at present; and by practice in singing he will be able to improve his voice [*per modum discendi plus sciet quam scit inpresentiarum de cantu, et per usum cantandi meliorare poterit vocem suam*]. Moreover, the said master and scholars, in speaking of his behaviour in study, and our neighbours in speaking of his good character when living at home, agree about him. He himself, the bearer of this letter, is worthy, as I judge, on the evidence of such high testimony, to be associated with your college.

"And now that he has been so recommended, I commend myself to you and to your prayers. I beg your Holiness to be pleased to absolve, and to commend to God, the soul of brother John de la Heeth, a name written on my heart.

"May God in His mercy vouchsafe to keep you all in safety."

Robert was admitted on November 11, 1323.

1028

A TESTIMONIAL TO A WORCESTER SCHOOLBOY

Folio 115, d. No. 1028. A.D. 1324

[The Prior writes to the Abbot of Westminster, introducing a boy brought up in the Convent.]

"We have found Robert de Henleye, clerk, the bearer of this letter, during his stay at Worcester at an earlier date, to be well mannered, peaceful, quiet; in fact, a boy of good disposition and praiseworthy life; so that thus, from boyhood's years, like a young offshoot from some beautiful flower springing up to perfection, and afterwards rooted in the garden of delights, the church militant, he has produced, to complete his virtue, the fruits expected of him. There can be no doubt that, starting from so virtuous a beginning, his character will justify the hopes we form of him."

1039

A CORRODY GRANTED TO A SPECIALLY HONOURED GUEST

Folio 117, r. No. 1039. A.D. 1324

THE Prior and Convent grant to John of Bitterley, who already holds a pension, " all necessaries for the rest of his life on honourable terms in food and drink, as to one of our chief clerks. Whenever from illness, or other cause, he is prevented from dining with the Prior or in the hostelry, and wishes to dine in his own chambers, he may have one monk's loaf, and one supper loaf for supper, and two gallons of the beer which the Convent is drinking, and from the kitchen on meat days a dish from the joint, and supper, and on fish days a dish from the best fish, and a pittance such as a monk receives from the commons in the misericordia or the refectory.

" His two attendants are to have every day from our cellerar two servant's loaves, two gallons of servant's beer, and from the kitchen what two of the Prior's grooms receive. If either is absent half of this allowance stops.

" We grant also to Master John the room in our priory situated next the Guests' Hall, which is called the Painted Chamber. If that chamber should chance to be occupied for a time by some magnate on a visit, he should have the chamber in the infirmary which Nicholas of Norton had, or some other suitable room for the time, and then return to the room named above.

" He is to be supplied with firewood by our cellerar when it is needed. He will have the stable next the cellar which is called the Drench-house, with hay and litter for one horse, and for his prebend one hop of oats or its equivalent every night. If John is absent they are not bound to make any provision.

"John promises to pay 10 marks a year out of his pension for this.

"Worcester, July 15, 1324."

1048

GAMBLING IN LIFE INSURANCE

Folio 118, r. No. 1048. A.D. 1324

One of the favourite ways as shown above of raising ready money was to accept cash payment in advance for an allowance to last for life.

Thus the Prior and Convent accept 40 marks from Richard of Cradeley, and in return promise to give him one *esterium*—that is, one bushel—of pure and dry wheat from the granary in the priory every Monday as long as he lives.

In 1051 John Flemyng pays £30, and has in return a monk's loaf and a gallon and a half of beer every day for life.

In 892 (A.D. 1320) Warin, the head porter, pays £25 to the Prior for his office and fees, and an allowance of food which is minutely described, and for assistance when he is too old to do his work.

In 948, in the year 1322, John de Bradewas pays besides ten quarters of wheat, 200 marks, partly in cash, partly in remitting an old debt, partly in land, and is promised a liberal allowance of food, and the use of St. Oswald's chamber for himself and a friend, and a stable for two horses, and hay and firewood. He is assured that he shall always have the best beer, one and a half gallons.

In 980, A.D. 1323, there is a very different arrangement. The Convent grant to William de Hampton, a chaplain, in return for 40 marks paid down, four quarters of wheat and eight of mixed meal or barley, one ox worth a mark, four pigs worth a mark, at Martinmas, and on the first Sunday in Lent 6s. 8d. to buy fish.

There is yet another variety. In 1097 we read that

1083

THE PRIOR OF ABERGAVENNY IS RECALLED TO WORCESTER

Folio 123, d. Nos. 1083, 1084. A.D. 1325

In the year 1320, as it appears from document 887, Richard de Bromwych, a learned monk of Worcester, had been appointed Prior of Abergavenny. He had received permission from the Prior to accept the post, "and to remain there continually." He had been "set free from all obedience" to the priors of Worcester. The following letter is, therefore, somewhat surprising:

"To our brother in our holy religion, Richard de Bromwych, the Chapter of the cathedral church of Worcester, that he may have the spirit favourably to consider and act on this that is sent to him.

"Our Mother Church, as of old she shines out more conspicuous than all her subject daughters with special beauty in its material structure, so, in the persons under her rule, soundly indoctrinated in the law of God and man, she has been wont to excel all others. But death, for which we weep, whose summons in the course of nature no mortal can disobey, has withdrawn from us some of them and left us few to look forward to. No wonder that for this reason we are struck with heartfelt grief, ever since the Word of God, which flowed among us like a stream, has, as it were by the bite of death, been withdrawn from us, and the stream dried up.

"Hence it is that after continual meditation on the subject of this great loss, and after weighing it from every side, we have considered that great outlay and expense was lavished on you; an expenditure through which, in process of time, you reached the summit of your Master's degree, that burden which for so long a time lay on you to be borne.

"For these reasons, in repayment for all these things, you are bound to put aside all other obligations, and return to our mother, who for a time and times has thus brought you up, although while she herself was silently calling you back, you transferred yourself too willingly to a distant place.

"As to this return, that it is due from you and becoming, we each and all equally are of one mind, praying you with deepest affection that after careful deliberation on this matter, you will without long delay be willing to return; so that the name and high reputation which our mother has hitherto inherited from the people, although for the moment clouded over, may be restored by your return, and that she may rejoice at its accomplishment.

"May Christ's mother, who will for ever live with Him above the skies, bring you back to us."

To recall one who had for some years been a prior, and reduce him to the rank of a monk, seemed to call for some special indulgence; and, therefore, the Convent invited his brother Henry to come and attend upon him. The terms offered are of some interest.

"The Prior and Convent, on account of the value of the character and conversation which we have long experienced and known in our dear brother and fellow-monk, Richard de Bromwych, *Sacræ paginæ professor*, grant unanimously to our dear brother in Christ, Henry de Bromwych, who will faithfully serve his brother Richard, a suitable chamber in the priory, and one boatload (?) [*navata*] of firewood from our undergrowth [*subbosco*] of Trumpeleye, food and

drink for himself, and for a servant such as the valettus of the Prior receives.

"By special grace, in addition to the food above mentioned, he may have daily one white loaf called the supper-loaf, and a pittance for supper on the days when he wishes to sup, when he takes supper as the Sub-Prior is accustomed to have it, apart from the common table. He may have a horse standing in the Prior's stable with sufficient hay, and half an *esterium* of oats every night.

"This is on the condition that nothing of the above is due to him except while his brother is present with us in person. When the said Henry comes to us as a guest we wish him to have *de victualibus unius treter* * *juxta exigentiam status sui.*

"When Richard has come to stay with us, and Henry also to serve his brother, he may have all as above stated. We also grant to Henry, wherever he stays in the future, as long as his brother Richard lives, a gown of the cut of the Prior's esquire, with fur, and a gown for his servant of the cut of the Prior's servants. If Henry should die in Richard's lifetime, or leave his service, Richard may choose another, to be engaged or dismissed at his pleasure: and if he should leave or die, Richard may choose whom he thinks best for his whole life, along with the servant in place of Henry's servant.

"All this is carefully secured, and provision made that by no means or contrivance [*machinatio*] Richard shall be deprived of the service.

"September 8, 1325."

* *Treter = traiteur or envoy.*

Note.—Richard did return to Worcester. In our library is a book (F. 62) *quem emit Henricus Fouke de magistro Ricardo de Bromwich quondam priori bergevencie pro xx. solidis.*

1098

LEASE OF A TENEMENT IN THE CEMETERY

Folio 127, r. No. 1098. A.D. 1326

THE terms of this lease, and the localities named, present some points of interest.

"The Prior and Convent grant by deed to Richard of Shrewsbury, innkeeper, and Cecilia his wife, for forty years a tenement in our cemetery of Worcester belonging to the sacristy of the church. In length it extends from the gate of the Bishop to the *celarium juxta scalarium* which John of Astley lately held of the sacrist; in breadth *secundum quod per edificia et palatia liquere poterit*; on the terms of the former occupant, viz. Richard and Cecilia are to keep it in good repair, and pay 1 mark in quarterly instalments; and they may not sublet or bequeath it. Should they do so the sacrist will enter and hold it. If they fail to keep the buildings in repair, or to pay the rent, the sacrist will enter on possession.

"If Richard survives Cecilia and marries again, and the second wife survives him, she will hold the property for the remainder of the lease on the same terms; and similarly, if he has children by her, his heir may hold the property. If all the above shall have died before the term of years expires, the sacrist shall hold the tenement with all its easements [*ediis*] and buildings for the use of his office.

"Signed by both parties in the presence of Nicholas of Pirier, Nicholas of Astone, Richard of Haukeslowe, John le Mercer of Worcester, John Blanket, and others.

"Feast of the Annunciation, 1326."

From the next document (1099) it appears that there was "at the end of High Street a *scalare* [stairs] of the cemetery of the Blessed Mary of Worcester."

1100

A VICAR RESIGNS HIS LIVING FROM OLD AGE

Folio 127, r. No. 1100. A.D. 1326

"SIMON, Vicar of Grimley, and of the chapel of Hallow, to the Bishop, greeting.

"Broken by weakness of body, ill-health, and old age, fearing to bear any longer the care of the souls in the parish of the church of Grimley, and the chapel of Hallow, as is becoming and right in me on account of the burdens resting on such a vicariate, I hereby resign purely, spontaneously, simply, and plainly this vicariate into your sacred hands.

"Signed and sealed by the Vicar, and also at his request by the dean of Worcester.

"Hallow, April 2, 1326."

1112

A PAPAL BULL AND ITS EXECUTION

Folio 129, d. Nos. 1112, 1113. A.D. 1326

"JOHN, Bishop, servant of the servants of God, to his beloved son the Prior of the church of Worcester, greeting and Apostolic benediction.

"William Galoun, clerk, of the diocese of Worcester, has complained to us that Richard Breton, Nicholas de Welnes, and John of Norton, priests, and Alicia de Almayne, a woman of the said diocese, disregarding the fear of God, have recklessly laid violent hands on him, even to the shedding of blood.

"We, therefore, by our Apostolic letter order your discretion, if the facts are so, to proclaim publicly that these sacrilegious persons are excommunicate without appeal, until they shall have adequately made amends to the sufferer, and shall have come with the testimony of thy letters to the Apostolic See to be absolved. But the woman may obtain from thee the benefit of absolution.

"Given at Avignon, June 4, tenth year of our pontificate."

1113

MEN AND WOMEN SUMMONED TO INQUIRE INTO THE FACTS

"The Prior of the cathedral church of Worcester, deputed by the Apostolic See as sole executor, to the discreet man, the dean of Worcester, greeting, and firmly to obey the Apostolic mandates.

"William, called Galoun, clerk, of the diocese of Worcester, has complained to the most holy father in Christ, by Divine Providence the Lord Pope John XXII . . . (as above).

"Therefore, by the Apostolic authority which we send to you to be inspected and faithfully to be returned to us by the bearer, we command you peremptorily to cite twelve men and women by whom the truth can best be inquired into, to appear before me in the cathedral church on the Wednesday next after the feast *sanctæ Fidis Virginis* (October 6), to declare on oath the truth which they shall have ascertained, and act thereon; and also peremptorily to cite the said William, Richard, John, and Alicia to appear on the day and at the place named to see, do, and receive what is just.

"October 10, 1326."

1115

THE ENDOWMENT OF A MONK IN A MONASTERY TO SAY MASS DAILY FOR A BENEFACTOR

Folio 130, r. No. 1115. A.D. 1328

[This is an endowment of a kind that has not hitherto occurred.]

"THOMAS, Abbot of St. Mary's Monastery, Bordesley, and the convent, make it known that since Master Henry de Hamptone, Rector of Lighthorne, in the diocese of Worcester, has shown favour and devotion to us and our church, we unanimously grant to the said Henry the support of one monk who shall for ever celebrate Divine Service in our convent of Bordesley for the soul of the said Henry; and that he shall, so soon as he wills it, present us a suitable clerk; and that after his death the Prior of Worcester shall so present.

"We bind ourselves and our successors to offer no hindrance, or malicious, false or frivolous objection. We assign to the said Henry one monk to perform this duty, until he shall have been promoted to priest's orders.

"For the clerk to be presented, and his successor, we will provide all necessaries down to his clothes and boots, and afterwards provide him as other monks.

"That this concession may be permanent we have caused it to be confirmed by our Chapter and the Chapter of Garendon. They bind themselves and their successors, and give power to the Prior of Worcester to enforce.

"Their own common seal and that of Garendon is affixed.

"Bordesley, feast of St. Simon and St. Jude (October 28), 1328."

1123

AN INTERESTING MANUMISSION BY THE BISHOP

Folio 131, d. No. 1123. A.D. 1327

THE Bishop sends the usual greeting to the Prior and Chapter.

"It is in agreement with reason that obedient and grateful sons should approve the deeds of their parents, and that well-disposed members of a body should respond to their head with the conformity that is due to him. We hope, therefore, that we may rely on your gratitude, by reason of which you have always acquiesced in our wish, as sons yield to their father, not to say to reason, and still more on your ancient affection, which we believe in such a request as follows weighs more than reason.

"Since then we have granted liberty to Osbert Spelly, our provost at Whiston, on account of the welcome and singularly meritorious service he has so long rendered to us and our church, we from our heart request and beg that you, so far as lies in your power, will in answer to our prayers favourably approve of this grant, so that both he, perceiving that it is by means of our common Church that he has been created out of nothing into a perfect man [*in virum perfectum de nichilo sentiens se creatum*] may with the more spirit devote himself to his rights and business; and that others, in hope of the like reward, may with the more vigour and fidelity discharge the duties entrusted to them. You know that, as we have explained to some of you by word of mouth, the completion of this business is for many reasons much at our heart. May you have strength long to observe our sacred religion and win its eternal rewards.

"Written in our manor of Hartlebury, August 2, 1327."

The following document (1124) records the deed of the Bishop that he grants to Osbert Spelly, of Claines, all the land and tenements with their appurtenances which Richard Spelly, Osbert's father, formerly held in villeinage in Claines, in our manor of Northwick, near Worcester, to have and hold, from us and our successors, for himself and the heirs of his body [*de corpore suo exeuntibus*] free from all service on payment of an annual rent of 14s. 8d. This deed is confirmed by Chapter, August 10, 1327.

1134

CORRESPONDENCE BETWEEN KING EDWARD III AND PRIOR: A CREDIT TO BOTH

Folio 133, r. Nos. 1134–1137. A.D. 1328

The King, writing from Randolf Lench, on June 22, in the second year of his reign, 1328, sends greeting to the Prior. "Our well-beloved Henry de Lichfield desires to serve God under the observance of your rule in your house, and we entirely desire that his wish in that matter may be speedily attained. We specially pray you to receive him as a monk in your house, and to treat him well and courteously as becomes your charity and love of us; and we shall be greatly obliged to you."

As no answer reached the King, he wrote again (1135), now from Burton-on-Trent, on July 16:

"We lately begged you to receive Henry de Lichfield into your house as a monk; to which letter, to our surprise and annoyance, you have not made any reply. We again request you to receive him, and to treat him in a good and courteous manner, or to signify to us why you are unwilling or ought not to do so; and we request you by your reply by the bearer to signify your willingness."

To this the Prior and Convent, after sending formal greeting, reply as follows (1136):

"Most honourable lord, we lately received your letter asking us to admit Henry de Lichfield as our brother in religion in your church of Worcester, and a second time, sire, you have sent us a letter for the same Henry. Most honourable lord, may it please you to know that we have inquired into the conditions of the said Henry in the places where he was born, and where he has lived. As a result we have been embarrassed in replying to your former letter, for which we beg your lordship to hold us excused. For this reason, most honourable lord, that we have found it certain that he is not suitable to dwell among us in religion in your church. We are assured that it is not your pleasure that he should be received among us, for that your church would be dishonoured by him, and less well served.

"May the High God, Who governs all things, grant that your royal power may long last in safety *a l'honeur de lui proeu*, and the salvation of your realm.

"Worcester, July 19, 1328."

The King receives this at Nottingham, and replies at once on July 23:

"We have well understood the excuse that you have made in your letter as to the receiving of Henry de Lichfield as a monk in your house, and we hold you excused for not receiving him for the reason contained in your letter."

1143

A SUMMONS TO THE GENERAL BENEDICTINE CHAPTER

Folio 134, r. No. 1143. A.D. 1328

"The Abbot of Ramsey, sole President for the General Chapter of the Order of St. Benedict in the province of Canterbury, to all abbots, and to priors who have no abbots over them, greeting.

"In the primitive church and in the ages that followed, at times when the ill-will of men was increasing, the holy fathers often put forward objections to meeting together in peace and tranquillity, for the advancement of the orthodox faith and the Christian Church, while the enemy of the human race was promoting disturbances and quarrels. These were objections to holding councils or chapters in the name of Christ, Who has promised that He will be in the midst of them through all the days, even unto the end of the ages, when even two are gathered together in His name.

"But afterwards the same holy fathers, when the Author of Peace granted them peace, with renewed joy making amends for past losses, met the more eagerly with fervent souls, and called on that Blessed Name which is above every name for grace and help in what they had to do.

"Since then for a long time past the English Church has had its peace disturbed, and has been grievously pressed and harassed, so that the Saviour of the Universal Church, unmoved by the cries of His disciples, has seemed not only to have been sleeping amid the stormy waves, but even to have deserted the ship ; and since the Lord has now provided most fit rulers, both in the temporal and the spiritual arm, so that the ends of the earth may see His salvation; now that divisions are hateful in State and Church; now that men, relying on God's help, are striving with all their might for that peace without which the Author of Peace cannot be rightly worshipped; the sons of the Church of England, and above all you who profess the Order of St. Benedict, on whom, after all the hardships and unjust persecutions of our sons the serene day of peace and quiet has, we may believe, already shone, ought to rejoice.

"We, therefore, strictly charge you to attend our General Chapter to be held on the Wednesday next after the feast of the Annunciation in the monastery of Abingdon, as decided by the abbots and others in the provincial council held in London. As the Chapter has not met for a long time you are bound to meet with the more fervent desire, to carry out measures for the good of the Order. Excuses for non-attendance are deprecated. This letter, when understood, is to be returned to the bearer who is our sworn messenger.

"London, February 20, 1328."

1144

A WOULD-BE MONK FAILS IN THE ENTRANCE EXAMINATION

Folio 134, r. No. 1144. A.D. 1329

DOCUMENTS 1134–1137 show that a man, even if the protégé of a king, could be refused admission to a monastery on ground of character. 1144, 1145 show that a suitable standard of attainments was also insisted on.

It will be observed that the candidate is described as a clerk. The standard, therefore, required for admission into the college of Worcester was distinctly higher than the pass examination which qualified for clerkship. The monastery was plainly in a position to choose among candidates for admission those who were most likely to do it credit. Admission for friends is solicited by the King, and bishops, and by authorities at the Court of Rome.

The Bishop of Worcester, Adam Orleton, writes to the Prior and Convent : " Since our beloved in Christ, Reginald de Thurlestone, observing that sound religion and the loving unity of brothers flourish in your monastery, earnestly desires to render devout service to the Lord there for ever in the habit of a monk, we urgently request you, at the instinct of charity, for his own merits, and through the intervention of our plea, that you will be pleased to receive him as a fellow-monk and brother.

" May the Most High keep you safe to advance holy religion, and grant you further gifts of saving grace.

" Beaumes, March 12, 1329."

To this request the Prior and Convent reply as follows:

"We have received your lordship's letter containing the request that we should admit, as our fellow-monk and brother, Reginald de Thurlestone, clerk, who desires to render devout service to God in our monastery, in the habit of a monk; and you plead the intervention of your request, and his merits.

"We must, therefore, by these presents convey to your lordship that, although we are rightly bound to obey your fatherly prayers and precepts in all matters where we can do so without incurring manifest danger, yet when we consider the merits of the said clerk, after examining him in literature and other things, as is our custom, we have found him incompetent to discharge the usual duties due to our church in Divine service. Therefore, to our regret, we cannot in this instance comply with your appeal; we are prevented by the insufficient qualifications of him for whom the request is made.

"May the Lord long preserve you to His honour and the wholesome governance of His flock."

1154

MEDICAL OFFICER RESIDENT IN THE INFIRMARY

THE following correspondence shows that a resident medical man had been for some time past charged to look after the health of the Prior and the Brethren, and that he slept in the infirmary.

Folio 135, r. No. 1154. A.D. 1329

" Let it be known to all that I, John de Bosco, clerk, hereby pledge myself to the Prior and Convent of Worcester, that to each and all of them, before all others, I will give advice and assistance and diligent and faithful attendance in the art and office of medicine; it will be, however, at their expense whensoever I shall have been lawfully called in [*requisitus*] through (per) any one deputed by them.

" I have also sworn on the Holy Gospels that I will not reveal their secrets however known to me, or those of the church, silently or explicitly, directly or indirectly, to any living person, or divulge anything that might prejudice them or their church, or involve any one of them in loss or scandal. Moreover, I have sworn that if I shall know of any one contriving evil against these my masters or their church, or of any evil otherwise threatening them, I will, to the best of my power, annihilate it, or warn them of it. In witness of all this my seal is appended.

" Worcester, December 2, 1329."

The following document (1155) states the terms of his appointment:

" Let all men know that we, brother Wulstan, Prior of the cathedral church of Worcester, and the Chapter of that place, have given to our beloved clerk, John de Bosco, as long as he shall live, in return for advice, help, and attendance to us and our brethren, in the art and office of medicine, given us hitherto, and to be given as often as through us he is suitably [*congrue*] called in, that he should receive from our cellar, every day of his residence with us, one monk's loaf, one *gustata* of the best beer, and from the kitchen both on flesh and fish days one monk's dish ; unless the Prior for the time being, or some brethren of the convent, like to invite him to dine with them, when they dine elsewhere than in the refectory or misericordia.

" If he then sups in the infirmary [*infirmitorium*] he should have a white supper loaf, and half a *gustata* of the best beer, and an honourable portion from the kitchen. While he is in residence his servant is to receive from the cellar and kitchen an allowance such as one of the Prior's grooms is accustomed to receive.

" We have granted him also a place for a bed in that chamber where other doctors [*medici*] along with the infirm have hitherto been accustomed to sleep, and the stable for one horse which Master Ralph de Wycheley has occupied, with sufficient hay and one hop of oats, or its equivalent, for his horse. We have in addition granted him 40 shillings of annual pension every year of his residence, to be paid him at the hands of the cellerar for the time being, at the feasts of the Annunciation of the Blessed Mary, and of St. Michael in equal instalments ; on the understanding, however, that if it should happen that the said Master John, or any one else at his instance, should be advanced through us to any ecclesiastical benefice, immediately from that time the aforesaid pension ceases.

" In testimony of all these things we have caused our common seal to be hereto affixed.

" Given in our chapter of Worcester, on December 2, A.D. 1329."

Note.—A *gustata* or *gyst* is defined more than once as a gallon and a half, Mr. G. G. Coulton has shown that the mediæval gallon was slightly smaller than ours.

1166

CAN A PRIOR, AFTER BEING ELECTED AND CONFIRMED AS BISHOP, RETURN TO HIS PRIORATE WITHOUT FRESH ELECTION?

Folio 137, r. No. 1166. A.D. 1330

THIS question arose under the following circumstances: On the death of Bishop Cobham in 1327 the Convent with leave from the King chose Wulstan their Prior to be their new Bishop; the King confirmed the election, and gave him the temporalities, and the Archbishop confirmed him, but did not consecrate him, as a rumour reached him that the Pope had reserved the bishopric. The story can be seen in Thomas's *Worcester Cathedral*, p. 169. The following letter of Adam Orleton, who was translated to Worcester from Hereford, will now be understood:

"Adam, by Divine permission Bishop of Worcester, to his beloved sons the Sub-Prior and Chapter of our church of Worcester, and to each severally of the monks therein, greeting, with the blessing and grace of the Saviour.

"Some time ago, when we were visiting you, we learned that some of you were unwisely distressed by a pernicious scrupulosity, hesitating whether you were bound to receive the commands of our brother Wulstan the Prior, and to obey him in matters which belong to the observance of the regular discipline, or to the administration of the Prior in things spiritual and temporal; inasmuch as he, on the last vacancy in the church of Worcester, created by the death of our predecessor Thomas, of happy memory, was by your agreement elected to be your Bishop, and confirmed by his metropolitan; and further that he, on the ground of this election and confirmation, exercised for some time, as is well known, episcopal jurisdiction in matters spiritual and temporal, and that he subsequently—on hearing that our Lord the Pope, long before that election and confirmation, had reserved the Church for the disposition of himself and the Apostolic See, and had translated us, Adam, then Bishop of Hereford, to the See of Worcester, and made us Bishop and Pastor of that church—on hearing this laid aside episcopal rule, and resuming the office of Prior, returned to his priory.

"We, therefore, noting that the said Prior, on receiving clear and lawful proof of the aforesaid reservation and translation, put aside all difficulties, entirely surrendered the administration of the See, and freely returned, as he could lawfully do, to his priory, and wishing to cut off all cause of hesitation, fearing lest through the vice of scrupulosity—a vice which sometimes creeps in among the religious owing to that prostitution of the human intellect which desires, contrary to the teaching of the Apostle, to know more than is right—that hesitation might lead to a revival of disputing, *ad recidivam disputationem ulterius deduci*, declare with pontifical authority that the position of our brother, and his return to the priory were canonical and lawful, and we hereby approve them; strictly ordering you, in virtue of your holy obedience, to show due reverence and obedience to our brother Wulstan as your lawful Prior, to lay aside all scruples of mistaken and curious inquiry, and in future support him in all spiritual and temporal matters that concern his office, as you wish to escape canonical punishment.

"Kempsey, November 10, 1330, fourth year of our translation."

ONE INCIDENT IN THE STORY OF DODDERHILL

Folio 137 (inserted leaf). No. 1168

Few parishes in the county have a more instructive and interesting history than St. Augustine's, Dodderhill. Much of it is known from other sources, and has been put together, but not published, by its late Vicar, Canon Price. But *Liber Albus* adds much to these materials; it contains more than thirty letters referring to it. I give here the last that I have met with; it is not dated except July 9. It was probably written in 1331, 1332, or 1333. The Bishop has been abroad.

"To the reverend father in Christ, Adam, the Lord Bishop of Worcester, his humble and devoted servants, Wulstan, Prior of the cathedral church of Worcester, and the Convent of the same place, with the obedience that is his due with equal reverence and honour.

"Your lordship knows that in waiting for a promise hope deferred maketh the heart sick [*spes que differtur affligit animam*], and all the more when hope has been long entertained, and delay brings danger.

"We have long followed with due diligence the proceedings down to the present day relating to the church of Dodderhill. We have incurred labour and heavy expense. We have waited long past the appointed times for the complete dispatch of the business promised us. We naturally fear that owing to the long absence of your fatherly care our own affairs and those of your church may be seriously prejudiced.

"We have thought it well to renew our respectful appeal to your lordship, trusting hopefully to your

The reply is given in 1184.

"The Prior and Convent of Worcester to the Abbot and Convent of Westminster, with the affection of brotherly love.

"Your letter recently addressed to us suggests two motives affecting the duty of mutually helping one another—namely, brotherly alliance, and our patrons' mutual affection in the Lord.

"In truth, referring to your second point, the holy mutual affection of the saints used to be consolidated by argument of deed rather than of word; and thus though whether there be prophecies, they shall fail, or whether there be tongues, they shall cease, their charity never failed.

"And as to the first point, wherein mention is made of mutual alliance,* let it be made known to your reverence by these presents that in all transactions with you, equally from the affection we owe you, and as a result of the brotherhood you speak of, we should act with equal grace and favour to your monastery and you, as far as we can, without offence to justice, and saving all the rights of our own church, did not the profession of brotherhood as established sometimes make it impossible, where after preserving in all respects its own rights, it has been able to rest content with a mere expression of thanks.

"Nevertheless when the affection of sons and

* This passage is obscure. "Reverentiæ vestræ presentibus innotescat quod in quibus [*erasion*] negotiis ex debito fraternitatis prefatæ affectu pariter et effectu monasterio vestro et vobis graciam faceremus pariter et favorem quantum justicia inoffensa et salvo jure ecclesiæ nostræ cathedralis predictæ possemus; si non initæ fraternitatis professio ex adverso nobis aliquotiens obviaret, ubi salvo sibi per omnia jure suo cum gratiarum actione potuit quievisse."

brothers has been on both sides consolidated, we do not say by words, but by deeds, following the example of our patrons in their mutual affection, the union will be firm, when brother standing aloof from brother shall have left to themselves those who lack the spirit of wholesome counsel. When this shall have been accomplished then without doubt brother will do for brother in this matter whatever without prejudice is in his power.

"May the Most High for ever keep you each and all in prosperity and peace.

"Worcester, November 10 (1331)."

1188

THE POVERTY OF THE NUNNERY OF COOKHILL

Folio 140, r. No. 1188. A.D. 1331

THE following deed of appropriation of the church to the Benedictine nunnery of Cookhill is interesting from its introduction :

" Adam, Bishop of Worcester, to his beloved daughters, the Prioress and Nuns of the monastery of Cokhalle, of the Order of St. Benedict, greeting, etc.

" It is acknowledged as a ground for blaming a bishop [*ad reatum episcopi noscitur pertinere*] if women, pledged as nuns to the worship of God, for whom the Bishop is bound to provide with fatherly care, are compelled by urgent poverty to desert their monasteries, and in order to supply the needs of the present to mix in secular affairs.

" From your own tearful statements we learned some time ago that owing to the unproductiveness of your land, the mortality among your cattle, the withdrawal of certain charitable gifts which you used to receive from the bounty of certain wealthy people, and other calamities, you were so oppressed by poverty that your monastery was on the verge of disastrous dissolution. You, therefore, humbly entreated us to grant you the revenues of the church of Bishampton in which you claim the right of patronage. We, therefore, after careful examination and consultation with our Chapter, formally make this appropriation.

" On the cession or decease of the present Rector they may by a proctor enter into possession. A suitable income is to be reserved for the Vicar.

"Withyndone, December 19, 1331, confirmed by Chapter, January 19, 1332."

It appears from 1095 and 1189 that the nunnery of Cookhill had to pay to Worcester an indemnity in the form of a pension of 1 mark for this gift, the payment of which was, however, delayed till the nunnery was actually in possession.

1193

A CHANTRY AT STRATFORD-ON-AVON, WITH DETAILS

Folio 141. r. No. 1193. A.D. 1331

JOHN DE STRATFORD, D.C.L., of Merton College, Oxford, a King's clerk, and Archdeacon of Lincoln, and for a short time Dean of Westbury, became Bishop of Winchester, Chancellor and Archbishop of Canterbury. When Bishop of Winchester in 1331 he founded a chantry in the parish church of his native town, Stratford-on-Avon. The deed gives unusual detail, and I give a translation of a large part of the deed. With the consents of the Bishop and Chapter of Worcester, of the Rector, and of all concerned, he founded, rebuilt, and endowed a chapel in the south aisle of the parish church at Stratford-on-Avon, in honour of St. Thomas the Martyr.

"The chantry is founded for my salvation [*salus*] for that of my brother Robert, for the souls of Robert and Isabella, our father and mother, for the welfare of Edward III, the Bishop of Worcester for the time being, and his successors, for the souls of deceased kings of England, of deceased bishops of Worcester and Winchester, and for the souls of brothers, sisters, parents, and other benefactors, the chantry to be served by five chaplains, if God grant it, for ever."

Of the five chaplains two are to be permanent; one of whom will be warden, and be placed over the other chaplains; and will be commonly styled Warden of the Bishop of Winchester's Chapel at Stratford. The other will be sub-warden. The remaining three will be temporary.

Then follow detailed arrangements for the appointment of the chaplains during the founder's life and subsequently, and for their maintenance; and many contingencies are provided for. The deed continues as follows:

"The Warden and Sub-Warden and the three other Chaplains shall live together, and spend the night in a manse provided for their occupation in the town of Stratford—namely, the Warden and Sub-Warden sleeping in one room, and the other three in another room, as arranged by the Warden; and they shall dine together, unless prevented by reasonable cause.

"The Warden shall find a clerk competent to serve them in celebrating Masses, and to serve them in their rooms: and he shall provide the Sub-Warden and chaplains with good surplices, and black amices fitted with black fur: these they should wear in the chapel, and in the parish church when attending Divine service.

"The Sub-Warden is to have charge of the books and ornaments of the chapel, and to arrange the celebrations; that is, he is to fix the hours and order in which he and the others celebrate, and to provide that bread, wine, water, and light shall be ready for Masses and for all Divine offices, at the cost, however, of the Warden.

"On Sunday and double feasts we wish that no Mass should be celebrated in the chapel, except with the consent of the Rector, before the Gospel has been read through in the high Mass [*alta missa*] in the parish church. And if all the chaplains cannot conveniently celebrate in the chapel after the reading of the Gospel, then some of them should celebrate at other altars in the parish church as may be arranged."

At this point orders are given as to filling vacancies,

and reporting expense. Then the deed goes on to describe the services to be performed.

"We desire and order that the Warden, Sub-Warden, and the three chaplains shall say together every day, after dinner and before Vespers, the Office of the Dead, viz. *Placebo* and *Dirige*, with the nine Psalms and nine Lessons, except on double feasts and at Eastertide. At Eastertide they are to say that Office with three Psalms and three Lessons according to the use of Sarum. After Vespers and Compline let them say in the chapel the commendatory of the dead.

"Before dinner every day let them say Mattins and the other canonical hours in the chancel of the parish church, along with the chaplains and clerks of that church, and also the seven Penitential Psalms and the fifteen Psalms of the Steps [*graduales*] with the Litany and the usual prayers in the chapel.

"All the chaplains are to celebrate their Masses every day in the chapel, if there is no lawful hindrance, as arranged by the Sub-Warden. Every Monday, however, one of them as arranged by the Sub-Warden, is to celebrate one Mass *per notam* (i.e. sung), with the office of the Dead for the souls of my father and mother and others named above, and for all the faithful departed, with the Collect *Inclina, Domine, aurem tuam*, etc. After my death for my soul, and for the souls of all named before, with this principal Collect, *Deus qui inter apostolicos sacerdotes*,* etc.

"On every Tuesday a Mass should be celebrated *per notam* of St. Thomas, sometime Archbishop of Canterbury. On Wednesday of St. Katherine, Virgin

* This is the beginning of the collect for deceased bishops or priests; it would contain the words *famulum tuum pontificali fecisti dignitate vigere*, etc.

and Martyr. On Thursdays of the Holy Spirit. On Fridays of the Holy Cross. On Saturdays of the glorious Virgin Mary, Mother of Our Lord Jesus Christ. On Sundays of St. John the Evangelist.

" All these Masses are to be celebrated each day *per notam*, with the Collects written below; unless on account of the solemnity of some feast, or for other just cause, the Sub-Warden orders that they be celebrated *sine nota*.

" The other chaplains are to celebrate every day *sine nota* for the departed, with the Office *Requiem æternam*, etc., along with the Collects indicated below. We wish that all the chaplains should assist [*intersint*] the celebrators of those Masses which are to be celebrated *per notam* in the chapel aforesaid.

" We also wish and ordain that the chaplains in celebrating their own Masses, as stated above, say in their separate Masses the following Collects or prayers.

" The chaplain who celebrates on Mondays the Office of the Dead *cum nota* should have as the principal Collect, according to the manner noted above, viz. *Inclina Deus* before our death, and after our death *Deus qui inter apostolicos sacerdotes*, etc., and before and after our death let them say six prayers.

" Before my death let there be the second Collect for our welfare, *Rege quæso famulum tuum*, etc.; for the king, *Deus in cujus manu corda sunt Regum*, etc.; for living brothers and parents, *Deus qui caritatis dona*; for peace, *Deus a quo sancta*, etc.; for the souls of all the faithful departed, *Fidelium Deus omnium Conditor*, etc.; and for the living and departed, *Omnipotens sempiterne Deus qui vivorum dominaris*.

" But after our death let the second, for father and mother, *Inclina Domine*, etc., be in place of the

Collect *Rege quœso*, etc., along with other Collects named above. Let all the chaplains who celebrate for the departed observe this order of Collects. Let the chaplain, however, who shall each day celebrate the special Mass according to the prescribed form in my lifetime have the second Collect *Rege quœso*, etc., and all the other Collects following, with this exception, that in place of the Collect for peace, *Deus a quo*, etc., let him say for my father and mother, *Inclina Domine*, etc., and after our death in place of *Rege quœso*, let him say the prayer *Deus qui inter apostolicos*, etc.

"We also wish and ordain that each of the chaplains, in their separate Masses *in memento* for the living, should have specially in mind the persons whose names are written below, as long as they shall live, viz. ourselves and our brother while we live, the Lord Edward our King, and all the Kings of England for the time being, the Lords Bishops of Winchester and Worcester; and that in the same *memento* let them specially entreat for peace in Church and Realm, and for all benefactors to the chapel, whosoever they may be.

"And in the *memento* of the dead, after our death, in the first place let them have in mind memory of us; then of our father, mother, and brother aforesaid; next of others named above, and of deceased benefactors to this chapel. Then of others, as it shall seem expedient, and for the souls of all the faithful departed.

"We firmly desire that all and each of the foregoing regulations made by us shall be observed in all and every particular; reserving, however, always to ourselves the power to add, correct, change, or diminish them as may seem to us more expedient.

"Southwark, October 8, 1331.

"Confirmed by Adam, Bishop of Worcester, *Bellum mansum*, February 21, 1332, and by Chapter, Worcester, March 12, 1332."

The ordinary duties of the chantry priest or chaplain on every day appear to have been as follows:

One of them sung in the chapel a special Mass, and the others were expected to attend. Then each in order successively celebrated his own Mass in the chapel, each with six Collects and a *memento*.*

They then attended Mattins and the other canonical hours in the chancel of the parish church, with the seven Penitential Psalms and the fifteen Psalms of the Steps, and Litany and other prayers.

Then followed dinner. After dinner they said in the chapel the Office of the Dead, *Placebo* and *Dirige*, nine Psalms and nine Lessons, all being present.

Vespers and Compline followed in the parish church choir; and finally the commendatory of the dead in the chapel.

Nothing, it will be observed, is said about teaching a school, and nothing about study.

It may be interesting to quote here from 1089 the conditions imposed in founding a chantry at Chelmscote, in a chapel of the parish of Brailes.

"The chaplain will faithfully celebrate for the souls named in the deed of foundation. Thomas (de Pakyntone, the founder) and his tenants and neighbours of Chelmscote may, if they wish, hear the daily Offices in the chapel, on condition that they faithfully perform all that is due and customary to the parish church of Brailes, and from it receive all the sacraments which pertain to Christianity. Thomas and his neighbours

* The *memento* is part of the Canon of Mass, in saying which the priest mentally inserted certain names.

aforesaid, on Christmas Day, the Purification, the Parasceve, Pascha, Pentecost, St. George's, All Saints', and the dedication of the church of Brailes, shall come, as is befitting, to hear the Church Service, and visit the Mother Church, unless prevented by manifest and reasonable cause; but on these days there may be no celebration in the chapel.

"Confirmed in Chapter, Worcester, September 30, 1325."

1198

VISITATION OF THE CONVENT BY THE BISHOP, SIMON DE MONTACUTE

Folio 143, r. Nos. 1198, 1199. A.D. 1334

NOTICES of episcopal visitations are rare in the *Liber Albus*: and these two documents, dating early in the Bishop's episcopate, are therefore transcribed with some abridgment.

The Bishop reminds the Prior that when he personally visited the convent he found some matters needing correction. They have not yet been attended to, and he is anxious for a speedy settlement.

"We, therefore, send to you our beloved clerks, John de Clipstone, our official, and Henry de Newbold, the auditor of our causes, and we beg you to rely on them as representing us in all that concerns that visitation, and to carry out, as soon as you are able, what they say; so that, in accordance with your reply to our clerks, such a remedy may be applied as we wish, to your advantage and honour and unity.

"May Jesus Christ in His mercy preserve you in prosperity.

"Written at Bredon, April 6 (1334), under our private seal."

1199

"To the reverend father in Christ the Lord Simon, by the grace of God the Bishop of Worcester, his humble and devoted brethren Wulstan, Prior of the cathedral church of Worcester, and the Chapter of the same place, filial obedience and reverence and honour."

and friends ; also for the souls of John de Sarn, the lady Sibilla his wife, and all their ancestors, heirs, and parents ; also for the souls of Walter de Beauchamp and Alicia his wife, and Walter, William, and Egidius his sons, and Petronilla his daughter, and their heirs, parents, and friends ; also for the souls of Simon of Crombe, his ancestors, heirs, and friends ; and for the souls of all the faithful departed, these Masses are to be sung in the parish church of Ripple."

To those who so celebrate or sing them he then grants the land, and makes in detail the necessary arrangements.

The endowments, and mode of presentation, the oath to be taken by the chaplains, and their duties are then defined. Every chaplain is to attend Mattins and the other canonical hours in the parish church, with the other chaplains and clerks.

"He is to say at the Mass while I live one Collect and post-Communion for me, and another similarly for the others named above ; and similarly after my death."

Rules are then given for conduct and correction ; for providing candles for their disposal ; for gifts of money and corn on the founder's anniversary and All Souls' Day ; and for each chaplain to leave money to his successor.

Then follows a list of the *principalia domus* which he directs that Philip and each of his successors as chaplain shall leave to his immediate successor. I give the Latin terms and the English equivalent, which is in some cases uncertain.

Principalia domus subscripta, videlicet, melius plaustrum vel carecta (a fairly good wagon or cart) ; *caruca cum pertinenciis* (a plough with what pertains to it) ;

a *hercia* (harrow); an *archa* (chest); a *tonellum* (barrel); a *cuva* (vat); a *cadum* (cask); a *tina* (? wine bowl or flask); an *olla enea* (bronze pot); a *patina* (plate); an *urceolum* (pitcher); a *craticha* (? gridiron); a *mensa* (table); a *forma cum trestellis* (a form with trestles); a *mappa* (cloth); a *tuellum* (towel); a *lavatorium* (washing tub or bowl); a *pelvis* (basin); a *scala* (ladder); a *ventorium* (winnowing fan); a *saccus* (sack); a *bussellum ad mensurandum bladum* (bushel for measuring corn); a *corbellum* (basket). It is added that in every instance the best article in the house at the time when the chantry falls vacant is to be left.

The King's licence is given in full, dated August 14, 1320; confirmed in Chapter the day after St. Wulstan's Day, 1336.

1202

APPOINTMENT OF REPRESENTATIVES OF THE CONVENT IN THE COURT OF ROME

Folio 146, r. No. 1202. A.D. 1336

THE following is an abstract only:

"In the name of the Lord, Amen. In the one thousand three hundred and thirty-sixth year from the Incarnation of the same, according to the course and computation of the English Church, in the fourth indiction, on the twenty-fifth day of the month of August, in the second year of the pontificate of the most holy father in Christ, and our Lord Benedict XII by Divine Providence Pope, in the presence of my notary public, and of the witnesses subscribed below.

"The men of religion, N. Mauricii, Sub-Prior, and Henry Fouke, monks of the cathedral church of Worcester, were personally appointed in the chapter house to represent the Convent in the most sacred Court of Rome, with full and explicit powers; and they appointed their beloved in Christ, Masters John de Walton, and John de Cleeve, clerks of the diocese of Worcester, with full powers, whether absent or present, whether jointly or separately."

A list of witnesses follows, and the notary states that he has reduced it into public form and signed it.

1204

HOMAGE CLAIMED BY THE PRIOR FOR A HOLDING UNDER THE CONVENT

Folio 146, d. No. 1204. A.D. 1336

"MEMORANDUM that on Monday next after the feast of the Exaltation of the Holy Cross, after great altercations and many *dies amoris* between the Prior and Convent of the cathedral church of Worcester of the one part, and John Godard, heir of Sir [*dominus*] Hugh Godard of the other part, respecting the homage to be had from the said John Godard concerning land which the same John claimed to hold from the said Prior and Convent in Little Aston in our manor of Newenham, at length the said John, induced thereto by good advice and conquered by reason, on the Monday next after the Exaltation of the Holy Cross, that is to say on the 16th day of the month of September in the year of Our Lord 1336, in the tenth year of the reign of King Edward, third after the Conquest, did homage to *dominus* Wulstan, Prior of the church of the Blessed Mary of Worcester in his manor of Crowle, in the presence of brothers Robert of Clifton, and Robert of Weston, monks of Worcester, Philip of Spetchley, Baldwyne of Hedingtone, *dominus* Thomas the Vicar of Crowle, and many of the household of the said Prior, and many others. And on the same day the said Prior took seizin of the said manor first."

The allusion to the household of the Prior at Crowle shows that the Prior of Worcester at this date had a residence there. It was a favourite residence of Prior More three hundred years later, and the house existed till the middle of the nineteenth century.

1211

HOW RENTS WERE ENFORCED BY EXCOMMUNICATION

Folio 147, d. No. 1211. A.D. 1337

"THE official of Worcester to the Dean of Kington and Vicar of Lockesley, greeting in the Lord.

"Since by the letters of Lord Walter de Cantilupe, of good memory, sometime Bishop of Worcester, it appears evidently that the heirs and successors of W. Bagod and John Curly, lords of the Vill of Lockesley, and of other holdings, both free and native in the same, are firmly bound for ever bound in 18 shillings to the Camerarius of Worcester, pledged to be paid to him at Worcester every year at the feast of the Purification in pure and perpetual alms; and since all and each of those who hold back the said rent unjustly are liable to the sentence of greater excommunication, as presuming to deprive the church itself of Worcester of its rights; we, therefore, straitly command you in virtue of your obedience in the church publicly and solemnly to denounce as excommunicate all those who detain the said rent, having summoned them in person to attend. This is to be done until you shall have received further instructions from us.

"Worcester, February 18, 1337.

1217

THE FOUNDING OF A CHANTRY IN EASTINGTON, WITH DETAILS OF SPECIAL INTEREST, BY A GOOD AND FAITHFUL LADY

Folio 148, d. No. 1217. A.D. 1338

"I, Isolde de Audeleye, expecting according to the Apostle that we shall all stand before the judgment seat of Christ, to receive joy or sorrow according to our merits or demerits, at the trial of the great and last judgment; and wishing, by my actions, as far as I can, to anticipate to my advantage the day of the final harvesting, and with mind fixed on things eternal to sow on earth seed from which when Our Lord returns I may gather fruit multiplied many fold, with glory in the time to come; wishing also so to dispose of the use of my temporal goods that they may both profit me in heaven as some slight help in matters spiritual, and on earth may provide welcome support to those nearest to me; for these reasons, with the consent by charter of our illustrious King Lord Edward hereto annexed, do found hereby a perpetual chantry at the altar of the Saints Thomas the Martyr and Katherine the Virgin, in the church of the Assumption of the Blessed Mary of Estyntone, in the diocese of Worcester, for the souls of Walter de Balun and Hugh de Audeleye, Knights, and for my health while I live, and rest for my soul when I shall have passed away [*migravero*] from the light, and for the souls of my parents, relatives, friends, ancestors, heirs, and benefactors, and all the faithful departed. A suitable chaplain is to serve the chantry which I have endowed from my domains, rents and income of my manor of Estyntone."

The King's charter follows in the usual terms, allowing Isolde to grant to the chaplains two messuages and fifty-eight acres of land.

"Dated *apud* Villam de Sancto Johanne, July 20, tenth year of reign (1336)."

Then follows a charter describing in detail the lands given by Isolde, and guarantees and witnesses.

And then follow further gifts.

"I have given and assigned besides the aforesaid messuages and lands to the aforesaid Adam the chaplain, and all the chaplains who succeed him in this chantry, one breviary [*portiforium*] worth 60 shillings sterling, one missal worth 4 pounds, one gilt chalice worth 30 shillings, two pairs of vestments worth 30 shillings, two pairs blessed altar cloths [*linthiamina benedicta*] worth 5 shillings, and two pairs of towels [*manitergia*] price 12 pence. Every chaplain on institution by the ordinary, and on induction by the Rector, is to swear that he will safely guard the ornaments aforesaid, and during a vacancy in the chantry they are in the charge of the Rector."

Then follow details as to filling up vacancies, and the duties of the chaplain are precisely defined.

Some other unusual and interesting regulations follow.

"The chaplain shall receive money from no one for performing any Divine Service, but he is to be entirely content with the portion assigned by me; and if one of them disobeys this order, on conviction he is to be removed, and another put in his place.

"If any one becomes so old or infirm that he cannot in person celebrate Mass, let him say private prayers, such as he can; and every week cause two Masses, one for the souls of Walter and Hugh, and one for me, to be celebrated with the aforesaid prayers, and for such age and infirmity he is by no means to be removed.

" Also every chaplain is to pass on to his successor, of his own temporal goods, 30 shillings."

Further regulations are made as to the supervision of the services and repairs of the building.

" The heirs of my domain of Estyntone should supervise all that has been said above, and take care that the chantry shall be served creditably, according to my ordering, for the honour of God, and for me and my soul, and the souls of the others named above.

" They are to take care that the house, buildings and enclosure [*clausure*] of the chantry are properly kept up, and do not through defect of roofing or aught else fall into ruin and suffer from neglect of the chaplains. And if by chance, through fire or wind, or in any unforeseen way, or through age, the buildings become ruinous, or in any way, without the fault of the chaplain, fall into decay, I desire and ordain, and as far as is in my power I place this burden on my heirs of the manor of Estyntone, that they rebuild and repair the buildings with their own timber and at their own expense.

" The Bishop is to inquire at his visitation, and if he finds that any have failed in their duty, he is to punish them properly, and if necessary remove the chaplain.

" Estyntone, February 7, 1338.

" Confirmed by the Bishop, Hartlebury, February 17, 1338.

" Confirmed by Chapter, February 24, 1338."

1219

THE STIPEND OF A VISITING MEDICAL OFFICER

Folio 149, r. No. 1219. A.D. 1338

THIS document is interesting as showing that the monks might dine sometimes outside the monastery and take their commons with them.

"The Prior and Chapter grant to their beloved in Christ, Master John de Logwarden, doctor of the art of medicine, for his faithful attendance, and health-giving advice to be given to us and to our brethren in the art and office of medicine, whenever for this reason he comes to us in the future as long as he lives, that he shall receive from our cellar every day that he spends with us one monk's loaf, one gyst [*gustata*] of the best beer, and that on both fish and flesh days he shall be served from the kitchen as one of our monks is served, either within or near the monastery, whenever he chances to dine with monks for their pleasure in places of this sort near the monastery.

"When, however, he dines in the Prior's hall, or elsewhere within the walls with any other monk, the allowance described above ceases. In that case when he sups in the infirmary [*infirmitorio*] or in a chamber he should have one white supper loaf, and half a gyst of the best beer, and a good dish from the kitchen. We promise him also a good chamber, which shall be assigned him as soon as is conveniently possible, a stable for two horses, and two attendants, and sufficient hay and prebend for his horses, and provision for his servants.

"Master John will also receive a payment of 40

shillings a year from the cellerar, a payment which will, however, cease if he or any one else at his instance is promoted to an ecclesiastical benefice.

"St. John Baptist's Day, 1338."

1227

IMMORALITY IN A VICAR CONFESSED AND PUNISHED

Folio 150, d. No. 1227. A.D. 1338

This is the only instance in the first 160 folios of this record of a charge of this kind.

It is a document declaring that whereas J. de E., perpetual Vicar of the church of A., had been seriously accused of adultery and incontinence; and had been brought before the Prior, as exercising archidiaconal jurisdiction, for lawful punishment; and had personally appeared at the appointed time and place, and had confessed the fault, and had undergone the canonical penance, and had completed it, the Prior had discharged him; and affixed his seal to this declaration.

1233

A CELLERAR TO BE RELEASED FROM SOME RELIGIOUS DUTIES AND TO HAVE THE SERVICES OF A CLERK

Folio 151, d. No. 1233. A.D. 1332

[Simon Crump was one of the leading monks in the time of John de Wyke, and was a *Notary*. The following document shows that he acted for the Convent in the Roman Court, and contains other points of interest.]

"To all the sons of Holy Mother Church whom this writing shall reach, Wulstan, Prior of the cathedral church of Worcester, and the Chapter of the same place, salvation in the Lord.

"That there are in heaven many and various mansions the authority of the Gospel testifies; so that at the disposal of the Lord Himself, whose Providence in awarding them makes no mistakes, there should be many degrees of reward according to the measure and varying need of merit. For there, as the Apostle says, each one shall receive according to his labour. We, therefore, wishing in our darkly shaded passage through life to be illuminated by the rays of the true light, and to follow as closely as we can in the footsteps of the Light from above, unanimously and spontaneously have granted to Simon Crump, our beloved brother in Christ, our fellow-monk of the aforesaid church, for that he, unsparing of the perils of his life, despising the manifold personal suffering [*sui corporis cruciatu contempto*], in journeyings often, in perils in the sea, and specially in the Court of Rome, has watchfully and effectually laboured on our behalf, as some reward for his labour that is past, and for what is yet to come, that he should have a clerk, viz. Robert de Wornesleye, provided for him to minister to him in the future.

"This clerk shall during the whole of brother Simon's life receive from our common cellar every day one distribution loaf [*panis dispensabilis*], one flagon of the best beer, such as given to the convent, and from the kitchen both on flesh and fish days pottage and dishes such as are ordinarily given to one of the monk's esquires. He shall also receive every year at the hands of the cellerar for the time being a clerk's gown such as the cellerar's clerk who has charge of his accounts usually receives.

"We grant also to brother Simon aforesaid some mitigation of the duties of the roll [*onus tabulare*] so that he shall be placed on the roll like any other member of the convent, but that for Mattins he should be named to attend only on feast days at which copes are worn [*festis caparum*].

"We wish that this concession should be made known to the whole community [*universitas*]."

1234

THE PRIOR WULSTAN CAREFUL OF HIS RIGHTS

Folio 152, r. No. 1234. A.D. 1332

ASSIZE held at Worcester before William de Sareshulle and John de Petto, justices, on the Thursday Epiphany in 6 Ed. III.

Inquiry whether John de Brymenhulle, chaplain; Henry Siket, baker, and Joanna his wife, unjustly, etc., treated the Prior John; Henry and Joanna swear that they have not wronged him. Others swear that they have, to the amount of 10 shillings.

Inquiry made as to the origin of the Prior's rights. It is sworn that in the time of Philip (1286–1296) the Prior in the reign of Henry the Prior held the property and has held it ever since.

Ruled that the Prior has the holding and is paid damages of 10 shillings.

1240

OXFORD STUDENTS RECEIVE HOSPITALITY FROM A BENEDICTINE MONASTERY

Folio 152, d. No. 1240. A.D. 1331

[In an order given by Pope John XXII, at the request of Edward III, for the appropriation of the Church of Tetbury to the Monastery of Eynsham, Oxford, is an interesting passage about Oxford students.]

" In the monastery of Eynsham, adjacent to the town of Oxford, in the diocese of Lincoln, situated on a public route, hitherto large hospitality has been shown to scholars of the University of Oxford, and the King's people [*gentium regiarum*], and the poor and other persons travelling, and flowing to the said monastery."

1257

PAPAL DISPENSATION FOR ILLEGITIMACY GIVEN TO CANDIDATE FOR HOLY ORDERS

Folio 156, r. No. 1257. A.D. 1334

[The Bishop of Worcester informs the candidate that a dispensation has been obtained.]

" To our beloved in Christ, John Mayel, acolyte of the said diocese of Worcester, salvation in the Lord.

" ' We have received on your behalf the following mandate addressed to us :

" ' To the venerable father in Christ, by the grace of God Bishop of Worcester, or his vicar in matters spiritual, Gaucelinus, by Divine compassion Bishop of Alba, salvation and sincere charity in the Lord.

" ' John Mayel, an acolyte of your diocese, the bearer of these presents, approached the Apostolic See and humbly prayed, that in spite of the defect in his birth from which he suffers, being born from persons not in wedlock [*de soluto genitus et soluta*], he may be able to minister in the Orders he has received, and be promoted to all other Holy Orders, and even obtain an ecclesiastical benefice though it has the cure of souls. He requests the Apostolic See to grant this of its compassion.

" ' We, therefore, with the authority of the Lord Pope, whose charge in this matter we primarily bear, send back to you this acolyte, committing to your circumspection to consider diligently all the circumstances affecting the suitability of this person which ought to be attended to, whether he is not an imitator of his father's incontinence, but is of good conversation and life; on which points we intend to burden your conscience.

"'You may first lay on him salutary penance for that without obtaining dispensation he caused himself to be promoted to the Order of acolyte otherwise than correctly, and absolution first being given for this you may then of compassion grant his request; on condition, however, that as the responsibility of the benefice, which, after the dispensation, it may be his future to acquire, may demand, he shall arrange to proceed to Orders at the statutable times, and personally reside in the benefice; otherwise the effect of this dispensation as regards the benefice to be null and void.

"'Avignon, 10 kalends April, eighteenth year of the pontificate of John XXII.'

"On the authority of this mandate we have caused diligent inquiry to be made by a number of trustworthy men, religious, clerks and laymen, sworn for this purpose, and presumably with full knowledge of the facts, concerning thy life and conversation, and whether thou hast been or art an imitator of thy father's incontinence, and concerning other matters affecting the fitness of thy person which ought to be taken into account; and by this inquiry we have found that thou neither art nor hast been an imitator of thy father's incontinence, and that thou always hast been, and still at present art of good repute for conversation and life, and that thy merits support thy claim to obtain the favour of this dispensation.

"We, therefore, the Vicar aforesaid, after diligently considering all the circumstances aforesaid, and after laying on thee salutary penance, for that without obtaining dispensation thou causedst thyself to be promoted to the Order of acolyte otherwise than correctly, and absolution being given for this error, we grant you a dispensation that notwithstanding the defect in birth you suffer from, being born of parents not in wedlock, thou mayest minister in the Orders thou hast received, and may be promoted to all Holy Orders, and may hold an ecclesiastical benefice even if it have the cure of souls.

"By the authority of this mandate, according to its power, form, and effect, out of our compassion we grant this dispensation.

"In testimony whereof we have caused to be made for thee this letter, fortified with the impression of our seal.

"Worcester, A.D. 1334."

1266

THE BISHOP CLAIMS THE RIGHT TO APPOINT THE SACRIST

Folio 158, d. No. 1266. A.D. 1335

[The appointment of the Sacrist belonged to the Bishop, but it often caused friction, and was sometimes disputed. In the following letter the Bishop, Simon de Montacute, claims it.]

HE writes to the Prior as follows :

" We have lately heard that some of your fellow-monks boast and affirm that they are able, if they please, to be admitted to the office of sacrist of our aforesaid cathedral church, and can by their light thoughts and words divert us from our wise intention, so as to fulfil their desires.

" We know that we are able by our rights to commit this office and charge when we please to any monk of our college whom we choose as suitable for it. But though we regard you all as both in temporal and spiritual matters fit for every good work ; yet more fully relying on the fidelity and industry of our beloved son Simon Crumpe, your fellow-monk and our sacrist, on whose work as we hope we may rely, we some time ago entrusted to this brother Simon, as an expert and specially fit for this charge, the care and administration and full exercise of this office with its appurtenances, as you may see more fully contained in the letter we sent him about it.

" Nor do we intend without reason to remove from this office, at any sinister suggestion, or at any prayers contrary to the interests of our Church, our brother Simon whom we regard as a faithful, diligent, and suitable sacrist, and we wish this to be known to all.

"May the Lord Jesus Christ direct and preserve you in sacred service to His honour.

"Alvechurch, January 26, 1333–1334, first year of consecration."

[See also 1283.]

1273

APPROPRIATION OF THE PARISH CHURCH OF KIDDERMINSTER TO ST. MARY'S HOSPITAL FOR FEMALE LEPERS AT MAIDEN BRADLEY (IN WILTS)

Folio 159, d. No. 1273. A.D. 1335

The Bishop of Worcester, Simon, writes to the Prior and Convent of the hospital for female lepers of the Blessed Mary of Maiden Bradley, of the Order of St. Augustine, in the diocese of Sarum.

" It is a bishop's special duty to assist those who are devoting themselves to the service of the poor and miserable. He must, therefore, protect all religious houses and their property, and most of all such houses as this of which we know that the inmates escape all public notice, being segregated on account of the offensiveness of leprosy. These leprous sisters are living a religious, poor and honest life, but by the mysterious will of God suffer continual pain. There is every evidence of the charity and devotion of the canons and brethren, of their good life and conversation and of their great hospitality, from well-known facts and from their popular reputation. We count it, therefore, a pious, humane, and praiseworthy deed to help these leprous sisters that they may not perish even more miserably from hunger.

" There are also great demands on their hospitality from their situation; and they have suffered also from losses of their cattle through pestilence. They have built a costly infirmary and offices, and have suffered grievous exaction and persecutions from the malice of this modern time, and have thus fallen into manifest poverty, and want. They cannot provide support for the brethren taking Divine Service, and for the leprous sisters, and the usual hospitality, and they need immediate help.

"When we consider that the parish church of Kidderminster, of our diocese and in your patronage, and which according to the taxation for tithe does not exceed 31 marks in value, was lawfully granted and canonically appropriated in ancient times to the aforesaid leprous sisters, a concession and appropriation acknowledged by several of our predecessors, and by W., a former Prior and the Chapter of our church; and that you owned the parish church of Kidderminster, from which you were accustomed to receive up to the half of the tithes of the whole church, and are at present receiving them; and that owing to excessive simplicity and ignorance of law they sometimes presented secular clerks to that church, to the prejudice and great loss of your house, and the said leprous sisters, all which statements are proved and notorious—

"We, Bishop Simon, following in the steps of our predecessors, wishing not to destroy their work, but rather to confirm it, after consultation with the Prior and Chapter, and full deliberation, and the consent of all concerned, do ratify and confirm the aforesaid appropriation and confirmation. And we declare that the church of Kidderminster, with all its rights and appurtenances, was from ancient times and still is canonically appropriated to the leprous sisters and those who have the care of them; and we order that after the death of John de Kersle, or on the vacancy otherwise occurring, it shall be in your possession.

"November 1335."

Some further details are added, an income of 25 marks being reserved for the Vicar.

1277

THE PRIOR COMPLAINS TO THE ARCHBISHOP OF THE LIES AND CUNNING OF THE PRIOR AND CONVENT OF GREAT MALVERN

Folio 161, d. No. 1277. A.D. 1335

"THE father of lies, the old serpent, who in order to overthrow man by guile cloaked the false under the semblance of the true, has now, as we have learnt, some skilled disciples, students of his wicked teaching.

"For certainly, father and reverend lord, the Prior and Convent of Great Malvern have had recourse to subtle tricks, that they may by falsehood subvert your right and ours of visiting them, while in truth they find little support; and, that the suit so long pending between them and ourselves both in England and the Roman Court—a suit, however, which in the opinion of one who heard it ought never on the application of one party, or by reason of delay on the part of the judges, have been taken to the Roman Court—may be finally decided there, they have detracted from your position as much as they can, and have suggested to the chief pontiff, as is plain from the citation, of which we transmit a copy to your reverence, that they are unable to obtain complete justice in England because of your lordship's power; and thus, with the fraudulent and concealed purpose of weakening your rights and ours, they argue under a cloud of words that the protection you give us is unjust.

"On these grounds, most kind father, with our pious prayers we entreat your Holiness that as your church of Worcester has hitherto, when troubles pressed us hard, found in you its most valiant defender, so now, to protect your rights and those of your church, you will be pleased to extend the arms of your support, and by your letters commend your cause and ours to your proctor in the Roman Court, and others of your council who reside there. For if their fraud, which thus finds its origin in what is false, forces the church of Worcester, which God forbid, to submit, they will, if they prevail, force you and your successors, against whom though indirectly the suit is brought, to submit to the same sentence.

"It is unworthy, most reverend father, to care nothing for your own brilliant prestige, when you can prevent its suffering loss.

"We will send, father, to the Court, before the date mentioned in the citation, whatever your reverend lordship shall direct.

"May the Lord Himself preserve you, reverend father, in prosperity and honour for His own honour and for the governance of His Church.

"Worcester, January 9."

1283

THE FABRIC IS IN THE HANDS OF THE SACRIST, WHO IS APPOINTED BY THE BISHOP

Folio 162, d. No. 1283. A.D. 1335

[The letter that follows contains one of the very few allusions to building and repairing of the Cathedral. It shows that it was in charge of the Sacrist, whose appointment rested with the Bishop. At this time the middle portion of the North side of the nave was being rebuilt.]

THE Bishop, Simon de Montacute, writes to the Prior and Convent:

"If you well remember, we wrote to you not long ago that we think all and each of you are competent for any good work; but having fuller confidence in the fidelity and industry of our beloved son, brother Simon Crump, your fellow-monk and our sacrist, we by our letters patent entrusted to him, as a prudent man, and one in our judgment most suitable for this post, the entire administration of the office of the sacristy. Nor, as you have now known for some time, do we intend to remove him from that office, since he has long rendered in it good and laudable service, without reasonable cause, as we have elsewhere written to you.

"But you, as we have lately learned, have appointed the said brother Simon as your cellerar, perhaps with at least an indirect intention to frustrate our wise purpose in this matter. For this reason we wish, by the tenor of these presents, to make it known to you, as we did before, that as long as your brother aforesaid is giving good and laudable service in hastening forward the building [*ad expeditionem fabrice*] of the church of Worcester our sponsor, we will not remove him from the office of sacrist because you have entrusted to him the office of cellerar, without some other clear reason.

" But we will allow him for a time to fill that office along with that of sacrist until you have provided for another cellerar, which we hope will be soon.

" We beg that, with a view to the glory of God, and your own furtherance, as you desire that in all your affairs to have the advantage of your brother's diligence, so for the advancement of the fabric already spoken of you will willingly assist our sacrist aforesaid.

" May you have strength and happiness in Christ and the Church.

" Written at Alvechurch, February 18, 1335."

INDEX TO PRINCIPAL ITEMS

INDEX TO PRINCIPAL ITEMS

The reference is to the number of the document

INDEX TO PRINCIPAL ITEMS

INDEX TO PRINCIPAL ITEMS

INDEX TO PRINCIPAL ITEMS

PRINTED AT THE COMPLETE PRESS
WEST NORWOOD, LONDON, S.E.